FOR MORE THAN A DECADE, Sharon Pincott has lived in the Hwange bush among The Presidential Elephants of Zimbabwe: a celebrated clan of wild elephants that she is devoted to and will do anything to protect.

She has formed one of the most remarkable relationships with wild, free-roaming elephants ever documented, yet her battles to keep them safe never seem to end. One minute she's cherishing incredibly intimate encounters with these gentle giants, the next she's accused of being a spy and then her name appears on a Zimbabwe Police wanted-persons list. While things often seem to go from bad to worse, this passionate wildlife conservationist relentlessly perseveres, in the face of overwhelming odds, to stick by the elephants s¹

Written with engaging humour and w. Africa's wildlife, Sharon recounts the e in the wilds bearable, as well as some force her to question her sanity

I0861089

Succeeding her highly praised book, *The Elephants and I*, this captivating collection of bush tales offers a further glimpse into the wonders, and grim realities, of choosing a life less ordinary, where the species that you look out for is different from your own.

Sharon Pincott was born in Queensland, Australia, and now lives in the Zimbabwean bush. She has dedicated the past 11 years of her life to the preservation and promotion of the clan of wild Hwange elephants known as The Presidential Elephants of Zimbabwe. Her accomplishments have been featured in *BBC Wildlife*, *Africa Geographic*, *Getaway* and *Travel Africa*. Her previous book, *The Elephants and I*, was published to wide critical acclaim by Jacana Media in 2009. An international television documentary about her work – titled *All the President's Elephants* – which was commissioned by Natural History Unit Africa, will be screened from mid-2012.

During the fifty years since I first went to Africa, I have collected or been given a considerable number of books written by those who have been to Africa but very few stand out in my memory as being exceptional. I was privileged therefore to be asked to contribute a few words to this very special book written by a great lady who writes with such dedication, feeling and passion for the gentle giants of Africa. ... [Sharon] writes as only someone who has Africa in her blood can, of the despair and the delights of the so-called dark continent. Wildlife deserves a better deal than it is getting from Man, the most lethal animal on the planet and when I leave Africa now after every visit I cry tears of joy and anger. Sharon's book will, I know, bring similar feelings to the reader.

DAVID SHEPHERD OBE, FRSA, FOUNDER OF THE
DAVID SHEPHERD WILDLIFE FOUNDATION, UK

Sharon Pincott is the Joy Adamson of Zimbabwe. It takes a very special person to battle the loneliness and isolation of the African bush. Sharon's passionate commitment to the Presidential Elephants – in the face of soaring political tensions ... – is contagious. We salute her courage and dedication. Her book gives rare and important insights ... This vivid, first-hand account ... is heart-breaking.

WILF MBANGA, EDITOR, *THE ZIMBABWEAN*

What a remarkable piece of writing! In *The Elephants and I*, Sharon Pincott takes us on an incredible journey into the very heart and soul of Africa, its natural splendour and, of course, the gentle giants that traverse the continent. Such a tale is long overdue. While many have been lured by Africa's wildlife and beauty, few have managed to capture this splendour with such finesse and grandeur. It is in the joy, the sorrow and the lonely reality of a country and a species in serious trouble that Sharon is able to remind us of what it was like.

JASON BELL-LEASK, DIRECTOR, INTERNATIONAL FUND FOR
ANIMAL WELFARE, SOUTHERN AFRICA

Sharon Pincott has written a memoir worthy of her elephant friends.
A very moving story.

GARETH PATTERSON, INTERNATIONAL BEST-SELLING AUTHOR OF LAST OF THE FREE

The Elephants and I is a poignant memoir... In this portrait of both bliss and dismay emerges a mighty heart on a quest for those who have no voice.

ZINTLE MAKENG, *CITY PRESS*, SOUTH AFRICA

Sharon Pincott had the courage to leave a cushy life ... the grit to stand up against [those] who looked the other way as the earth's largest land mammals were slaughtered ... But perhaps what took the most pluck was for her to write this story openly ... if everyone had the spunk of Sharon Pincott we would have few conservation problems on our earth.

DELIA OWENS, PH.D AND CO-AUTHOR OF THE INTERNATIONAL BEST-SELLER CRY OF THE KALAHARI

A heart-rending story, set in difficult times: Sharon Pincott exudes passion, courage and dedication as she tells it like it really is. And there's still room for humour amongst the tragedy – you'll be inspired!

NICHOLAS DUNCAN, PRESIDENT, SAVE FOUNDATION OF AUSTRALIA

Sharon's story speaks of a genuine passion and enthusiasm for her new African home – joy at discovering a new world ... While the tale of a modern girl giving up city life for the faraway African bush is a few decades past qualifying for remarkable, it is lifted by the fact that she chose to swap a secure life in suburban, comfortable Australia for one of increasing political uncertainty in Zimbabwe ... finding herself pitted against land-invading 'settlers' and snares while seeking to protect her increasingly persecuted elephants. This [book] is for those who look out of the window at work, wondering 'what if' they pursued their dreams.

ANGUS BEGG, CNN AWARD-WINNING JOURNALIST/TV PRODUCER, SOUTH AFRICA

After reading [this] book you will feel as though you have been to Africa and experienced the wonderful world that it truly is.

ROB FABER, MANAGING EDITOR, THE ELEPHANT, THE NETHERLANDS

The Secret meets Born Free in this story of an Australian woman's bond with 'The Presidential Elephants of Zimbabwe' and her efforts to stay positive and protect them in a time of political upheaval, poaching and land invasions ... Final impression: a courageous and determined conservationist outlasts fear and intimidation to stay on and fight for her beloved animals.

BRITISH AIRWAYS COMAIR MAGAZINE

Sharon Pincott's The Elephants and I masterfully combines a tale of the struggle to conserve Zimbabwe's 'Presidential Elephants' with a portrait of what life in Zimbabwe is like; it is a passionate and touching read.

BIG ISSUE, SOUTH AFRICA

... Sharon Pincott is a remarkable woman; courageous, stoic, determined and resourceful. Her story of her trials and tribulations, and the fun times, in Zimbabwe makes good reading.

DAVID HOLT-BIDDLE, SOUTH COAST HERALD, SOUTH AFRICA

Battle for the President's Elephants

Life, lunacy and elation in the African bush

Sharon Pincott

First published by Jacana Media (Pty) Ltd in 2012

10 Orange Street
Sunnyside
Auckland Park 2092
South Africa
+2711 628 3200
www.jacana.co.za
Job No. 001725

ISBN 978-1-4314-0359-2

Set in Sabon 10.5/15pt
Printed and bound by Ultra Litho (Pty) Ltd Johannesburg

A portion of this text appeared in a different form in two self-published Zimbabwe-only-edition books of journal entries: *In An Elephant's Rumble* and *A Year Less Ordinary*.

Cover photos © Natural History Unit (NHU) Africa

See a complete list of Jacana titles at www.jacana.co.za

*For all of those who love
wildlife as I do*

Contents

Preface

An elephant calf was born one day in October 2008 and I christened him Masakhe. It's an isiNdebele word – the native tongue of the local Ndebele people – that means 'to build' or 'to rebuild that which has been broken'. Many things had been broken since my arrival in the African bush in 2001, when I moved to the unfenced land bordering the Main Camp section of Zimbabwe's Hwange National Park. Many things were still broken at the time of Masakhe's birth and I knew that, inevitably, more things would be. It was Zimbabwe's way. Yet it seemed like the right time to try to rebuild my African life, to help my elephant friends rebuild theirs, to focus on the good times and move positively forward.

It was never going to be smooth sailing. Although tranquility awaits every short-stay tourist it can, in reality, be an illusion for some residents – especially those who go into battle for animals that are unable to speak for themselves.

I am where I am today as a result of a series of events that took place in the early dawn of the new millennium when I was still living in Australia. My wildlife warden friend, Andy, was killed in a helicopter crash in the autumn of 2000 while he was tracking rhinos in Hwange National Park. I attended a seminar with fellow Information Technology professionals in the winter of that same year and found myself profoundly inspired to take more risks while on this earth – and to leave a lasting legacy. An 18-year relationship with my very best friend had also come to an end. The fact that she was a fluffy, four-legged canine made this no less poignant.

So, as the flowers of spring bloomed I sought a radical change, and found it as a volunteer working with elephants in wild Zimbabwe. By

March 2001 I'd traded my privileged First World existence to start my new life with The Presidential Elephants of Zimbabwe – the country's flagship clan of over 450 wild elephants. I knew nothing of Zimbabwe's ways; I was unpaid, untrained, self-funded and arrived with the starry-eyed air of most foreigners.

I have lived in the Hwange bush for more than a decade now, through good times and bad. It's been an unforgettable time, although I never imagined that I'd have to learn to contend with the awful consequences of poachers, sport-hunters, land claims, threats, intimidation, land degradation and indifference. I've already written about many of these battles in *The Elephants and I* – the story of my first seven years among the Presidential Elephants.

Sadly, although predictably, there are always alarming annual events that bear witness to the harsh realities of striving to preserve and promote Zimbabwe's unique wildlife. It's been said that if you're a wildlife conservationist in Africa and you *haven't* got someone after you, then you're probably not doing your job properly. This is perhaps true, and it is the price that I pay. Such episodes continue to plague, and alter, my life among the elephants and other animals.

In order to 'rebuild that which has been broken' in my African life, and to enable me to cope with the endless battles associated with keeping the elephants safe, I find that it helps to recall the more light-hearted, serene and innocent times that I've savoured among Africa's diverse wildlife. Times like these do, after all, motivate me to stay. So I've chosen to now share my stories of these fun and rewarding times, together with other tales about my surroundings and cherished relationships with elephant and human friends. These shed light on why I stay, and how I manage, despite the realities of the more ludicrous episodes, also included.

In this wondrous world of the leathered and feathered, I choose not to allow the preposterous incidents to eclipse the beauty and unique splendour of day-to-day life in the African bush, which deserves to be celebrated with a laugh.

Saving precious lives

No day is ever the same in the African bush. Despite not knowing what joys and sorrows lie ahead, there's always a multitude of both to be had. Although this day in May 2010 dawned like any other, it turned out to be an especially memorable one.

I'm forever on the lookout for snared animals as I go about my daily elephant monitoring on the Hwange Estate and as luck would have it I stumbled upon a badly injured female elephant. She was wandering on the estate without any members of her family and was struggling to walk. The snare wound on her back right leg was horrific and the deadly length of copper wire was clearly visible.

I'd resorted to buying a mobile phone only a few months earlier. Signal had finally become available on the estate, although, like many things in Zimbabwe, it was not yet reliable. I hated the possibility of the contact-me-anytime intrusion, but it proved to be a godsend when occasions like this arose.

I remained with the snared elephant and immediately phoned two nearby animal darters, who responded without delay. The elephant obligingly stayed in the open, away from thick bush and other elephants, which was an ideal opportunity for darting.

Although it felt like an eternity to me, the necessary equipment had been collected with haste and a dart promptly prepared. (The expensive M99 immobilisation drug is a vital prerequisite to an operation such as this, and is fortunately provided in ample quantities by kind donors.) I was able to drive the darter close enough for a shot, and the dart hit its target, but tragically the immobilisation drug didn't inject. Frightened by the sting of the dart, the elephant hurried off into thick bush.

It took time to prepare and load another dart and, as it turned out, a second chance didn't present itself. Not realising that we were trying to help her, the elephant had disappeared deep into dense bush where we could no longer reach her. It was one of those heartbreaking moments that I have so often experienced in the African wilds.

Although I had known immediately that she must be a Presidential Elephant – given her calm demeanour and close acceptance of my 4x4 – I hadn't been able to positively identify her. The elephants that roam the Hwange Estate became known as The Presidential Elephants of Zimbabwe after President Robert Mugabe issued a 'special protection decree' in 1990, as a symbol of Zimbabwe's commitment to responsible wildlife management. To make identification easier, I'd assigned a letter of the alphabet to each extended family group, and had given each elephant within the family group a name beginning with that letter. Based on this particular elephant's looks and body shape, I suspected she was from the A family. Back in my rondavel that evening I flicked through identification photographs, comparing tusk and ear patterns to the photos I'd just taken, and discovered that it was Adwina who was so horribly injured and wandering alone out there in the darkness.

The following few days in the field were particularly distressing. I searched and searched and couldn't find her anywhere. In the early hours of the morning, lying awake and reliving the misfortune of the failed darting attempt, I found myself wishing that I hadn't established her name. It's so much more personal when you know someone's name.

Petrol was horribly expensive at US$1.40 a litre, and my 30-year-old 4x4 managed only 4 kilometres to the litre, but how can you put a price on an innocent animal's life? So, I drove for more time and distance than I usually would each day, digging deep into my own savings.

Long weeks passed. There'd been no sign of Adwina. There were days when I thought she must be dead. Even so, I double-checked every female of her size that I came across, to ensure that it wasn't her. The rains were over and elephant sightings were increasing, but her time was running out.

More than a month after the initial sighting, I left for my daily round of patrols and monitoring in the late morning. Just the day before I'd declared, 'I'm going to find her this week', not actually believing it myself. I'd been in the open area called Kanondo for almost an hour when I saw Adwina's head in thick bush. At times like these I become a bit of a basket case. My heart pounds and my hands shake. I fumbled with my mobile phone …

Esther and her husband Hans, who were attached to the nearby Painted Dog Conservation Project, had successfully darted a horribly snared Presidential Elephant just a few months before, and were on standby. I'd actually had Esther on standby for weeks.

'She's finally here Esther, at Kanondo,' I blurted into my mobile, pretending to be calmer than I was. This wasn't the time to talk as they needed to pack their 4x4 and race the 15 kilometres to join me. There's never any time to waste with these operations, since the chance of the animal disappearing into thick bush is always high.

Only a few minutes had passed, but I was back on my mobile again. 'Esther, she's already moving off,' I warned. Thankfully, they were already on their way. By strategically positioning my vehicle in Adwina's path, I tried to encourage her to stay put.

Momentarily, I'm back on my mobile again, 'I'm not sure that I can hold her much longer. Please, we need a tracker …' I circle around and keep herding Adwina back and forth, back and forth, trying to prevent her from crossing the road into thicker bush. In desperation I phone for another vehicle to help keep an eye on her.

The vehicle eventually arrives, but it's just too late. Adwina runs across the road that I'm on. I can hear Esther's vehicle pulling up and I drive madly towards her, needing to get to the next road to prevent Adwina from crossing *that* one as well. Hans is driving and Esther is as calm, cool and professional as always, which does nothing to soothe my own thumping heart. Thank goodness one of us is so composed. She's about to start preparing the dart (the drug is potentially deadly if spilled on human skin, so I'm thankful that I'm not the one loading it) and has a tracker on-board. I leave them to get on with it and zoom off towards the next road.

By the time the dart and gun are ready Adwina is still somewhere between these two sandy roads. But the bush is horribly thick. We're all looking in the wrong direction when she eventually crosses. I catch a glimpse of her, however, and manage to confirm that it's Adwina. Mkhalalwa, our tracker, quickly leads Esther and Hans after her on foot.

It proves fruitless. There are sounds of elephants everywhere, and the risk of walking straight into one in the thick bush is high. Eventually, I see all three helpers retreating back towards the vehicles. My hands fleetingly cover my eyes in disappointment. 'We just can't miss her *twice*,' I whisper to myself. Yet it looks as if we have. It's not practical for this darting team to wait around too much longer, since the chances of Adwina returning to the open area of Kanondo are low. If some of the elephants we can hear are her family there's a chance that she will but, although we wait for a while longer, all we encounter are lone bulls.

Eventually, I return to Kanondo alone in the desperate hope that she reappears. A game-drive vehicle arrives with American tourists on-board, so I show the safari guide the gruesome photographs that I've just taken of Adwina and ask him to keep a close eye out for her.

Meanwhile, the Ws – one of my favourite families – have appeared in the open, sent perhaps to ease my despair. There's also a bateleur in the sky, which some believe is a spirit messenger. I immediately think of my dear friend Andy who lost his life while he was a wildlife warden in Hwange National Park. It seemed impossible that he'd been dead for ten years. 'Please help us find her,' I whisper, looking skyward, hoping that he can hear me.

I drive with the tourists to the mineral licks, where well-known elephant ladies named Whole, Whosit, Willa, Whoever, Wishful and others enjoy the minerals and then surround our vehicles. I share information about their intimate family relationships and introduce the tourists to all of my favourites. I explain that the elephants are very familiar with me and my vehicle and know my voice well, but that as strangers they must sit in silence and never attempt to touch or feed them. The Americans are visibly moved by their close encounter, revelling in their astonishing proximity. 'I could just cry,' a middle-aged man whispers with sincerity.

This makes me smile. It's the incredible effect that these trusting giants so often have on people. We talk some more about this remarkably friendly W family and also about Adwina and the darting attempt. Then, without warning, Adwina appears in the open just a few hundred metres away, about to splash soothing mud on her wound. 'Thank you, thank you,' I whisper instinctively, gazing once again towards the sky. If I thought my heart was pounding earlier it was now about to jump out of my chest. One phone call and Esther, Hans and Mkhalalwa are immediately on their way back.

Adwina does it to me again though. She starts to move off well before the darting team can get to me. I dash back to the same road that I was on earlier, having asked the safari guide and his guests to remain still and monitor her from there. Once again I herd Adwina back and forth, back and forth, trying to keep her from disappearing into the dense bush. But it feels like I'm going to lose her yet again.

I hear Esther's vehicle roaring towards us and at the same time get a glimpse through the bush of the safari guests waving coloured cloth in the air, someone's sweater perhaps, to help guide the way. Hans can now see where Adwina is, even though there are scores of elephants in the area by now, and he drives towards her. Esther knows that I'm struggling to hold Adwina at bay and, like me, fears that we'll lose her again if she crosses the road. She has one chance to successfully get the dart in and it's not a very good one since she's awfully close to the limit of the dart gun's 40-metre range and the thick bush is preventing her from getting any closer. Adwina isn't staying still, but with calm skill Esther leans out the window of her 4x4 and fires. The dart hits, albeit a little precariously, on the side of Adwina's leathery rump.

Through the leafy bush I can see the pink-feathered dart protruding from her backside and breathe a huge sigh of relief. My mobile rings and it's Esther confirming that the dart's in, and asking me to keep up with Adwina to see where she falls; assuming that enough of the drug has been injected to bring her down. Esther sounds cool and confident, as always. Adwina's head and trunk eventually start to droop and I'm thinking, peering at my trembling hands, that I could do with a bit of immobilisation myself.

In a few minutes she's down. We hurry in our two vehicles towards her fallen body and the operation is immediately in full swing. There are elephants all around us, but fortunately none are A family members and they're considerately keeping their distance. The injury is more than horrific. The length of copper wire is embedded deeply, and the wound is a great deal worse than it was a month ago. There's no skin left on the lower portion of her leg. Esther and Hans cut the wire and treat the wound. I tip water over Adwina's ears to keep her temperature stable and Mkhalalwa holds her trunk, ensuring that her breathing is not obscured.

I invite the game-drive vehicle to come in quietly, to witness this life-saving procedure. They are moved, of course, and the emotion is palpable. The wound is soon treated and we all move off so that Esther can safely administer the reversal drug alone. My whole body is shaking; it's impossible for me to relax until Adwina's back on her feet.

And soon she is. It's taken less than 30 minutes from the time the dart hit to seeing her standing once again. Five long weeks of searching, but just minutes of compassionate teamwork once I'd found her. Adwina wanders off, a little dazed, across the road that she's now welcome to travel without interference from me. Her family's still nowhere in sight, nor is her youngest calf, but I feel confident that she'll be okay. The resilience of these animals is remarkable. So long as the deadly wire is removed, the chance of a full recovery is high no matter how dreadful the wound.

It's a time for celebration and we all sit in our vehicles next to a pan, full of water from the generous wet season, surrounded by the W family who choose to stick around and seem to want to help us celebrate. Esther's gift from me is the opportunity to meet the beloved Whole – one of my most favourite elephant ladies. It is Whole's adult daughter, the cheeky Whosit, however, who insists on standing right beside Esther's open window.

I stayed out longer than the others, alone under the almost-full moon, sipping a beer handed to me from the game-drive vehicle's cooler box. I don't particularly like beer but, with my heart *still* pounding, something alcoholic was definitely needed. It was a truly stunning, and gratifying, evening. Whosit's firstborn, Wish, placed his trunk right inside my open window and proceeded to give my 4x4 a little shake. A tad naughty perhaps, but it made me laugh out loud just the same. This little Wish, who was only a few months old at the time, was an adorable mischief-maker. That evening I made my own wish – that we'd never have to do another snare removal. That wish, tragically, never comes true no matter how often I make it.

A few days later, while I was out with safari guests from Australia, we stumbled upon Adwina at Kanondo, splashing mud on her de-snared leg. She was still without her family, but she was looking much better than she had been. The back portion of her wound was horribly deep and raw, and a little blood still oozed from it, but she could now put her full weight on the leg.

It was another three weeks before I saw Adwina again, and by then she'd reunited with her four-year-old son. This was a really positive development since her youngest no longer needed to be looked after by family members. Having lost so much skin on the lower portion of her leg, there was nothing to protect the flesh and her wound was taking a worryingly long time to show signs of real healing. She mud-bathed and dust-bathed continually, helping Mother Nature along.

The next time I saw Adwina she was still limping – the merciless acts that humans are capable of very evident – but she was surrounded by all the members of her family.

* * * * *

Tragically, we don't always manage to save snared elephants.

A Hwange National Park elephant family that was frequenting Kanondo had a young member – about four years old – with a tight wire wrapped around his little head; his ear awfully damaged and the cruel wire cutting into his throat. Try as we might, a darting opportunity kept eluding us. They were a family of seven not known to me and, unlike the Presidential Elephants, they were particularly skittish around vehicles.

My short time observing them from a distance teaches me many things. Five different Presidential families, all of whom I know well, come and go around them. Still they stay motionless in the shade of a tree. 'They're waiting for somebody,' I mutter to the darter who's seated beside me in my 4x4.

Just a few minutes later a second National Park family materialises from the bush; it's one that I do sight now and again during the course of each dry season. Sure enough there's a greeting ceremony. The intensity of it tells me that they're not immediate family, but probably 'bond group' members who don't *always* roam together. There's no twirling of trunks or rubbing of faces, although they're clearly related to some degree and certainly excited to see each other. They back into one another, and open-mouthed deep rumbles fill the air.

The darter mistakes this commotion for hostility, which is easy enough to do. Unless you know and understand the interactions and associated sounds, aggression and greetings can be easily confused. What we had just witnessed was friendly fraternising. The small family of 7 had, all of a sudden, become a group of over 30, which complicated the darting procedure further.

'How closely were all of these elephants related?' I wondered. Would everyone in this extended group become concerned and protective if the snared calf was immobilised now? Without a documented history of past encounters, it was impossible to know. Even the mother of the snared youngster isn't easy to determine absolutely, with such limited observation time. He suckles from nobody, the snare perhaps making the suckling position painful. He belongs to one of two females, but which one? I make an educated guess, but what if I'm wrong? For security reasons, should the one who I think is the mother also be darted? With a four-year-old son, she is almost certainly heavily pregnant. With no records of oestrous periods or matings for this unknown family though, this is also just another educated guess. What negative effect might the drug have on a baby about to make its appearance into this world?

Darting youngsters in strange, unhabituated family groups is always a concern. Many things can go wrong and there are so many unknowns. My head spins with all that needs to be weighed up, and the darter is understandably hesitant. All of a sudden the elephants make the decision for us: they dash unexpectedly into impenetrable bush, and the darting opportunity is lost for the day.

I never saw this elephant family on the estate again. Unless a miracle happened and the snare somehow broke off without intervention, this family would have mourned the tragic death of one of their own.

Fortunately, other sightings have happier endings.

One afternoon I noticed a tiny six-week-old calf with a tight snare around its neck. This was the fourth member of the T family that I'd witnessed with a snare. I immediately called for darting assistance and an experienced darter named Roger (who was key in helping Esther become the skilled darter that she is today) responded. He was soon with me in my 4x4, dart gun loaded, leaning out of the open passenger window.

This young Presidential Elephant, as yet unnamed, was the daughter of an elephant I'd named Trish. With them were Tarnie, Teeka, Trudy, Tabitha and others from the well-known T family. Roger decided that with such a young calf he needed to dart both calf and mother. Having had no experience with a snared elephant this young, I didn't argue, although we'd only ever darted one other Presidential Elephant mother while removing a snare from a calf. Because all of them had been older, and I knew the relationships and the elephants well, it hadn't been necessary.

Roger took aim. I took an audible deep breath and involuntarily clasped my hands to my face. Roger glanced over at me, slumped behind the steering wheel, and said simply, 'It'll be alright.' The first dart hit the baby. The next dart hit the mother. Startled by the sting of the darts, both elephants immediately started to move off.

We followed behind them in a forest of acacias and I feared a flat tyre from the carpet of thorns. The baby was down soon, though, and to our mutual horror Trish instantly tried to pick up her fallen baby with her trunk. She managed this successfully and then unintentionally dropped the tiny one to the ground. 'I'm driving right in there,' I blurted anxiously to Roger, 'before she picks her up again and accidentally drops her from a greater height.' Roger had seen this happen before. There was also the risk that Trish, who had a dart in her own rump, would fall on top of her immobilised baby if we didn't force her to move off.

I put my foot on the accelerator and didn't stop until Trish and the two family members that were supporting her, were literally centimetres from my bonnet. I revved the engine, held one hand on the horn, and banged loudly on my door with the other, yelling at them. It was a horrible thing to have to do as these elephants trusted me, but I had no choice. They ran off hesitantly, leaving the immobilised baby on the ground beside us. Roger was already out of my vehicle, crouched behind the open door, snipping the deadly snare that would have strangled the growing baby within weeks.

As it happened, it probably hadn't been necessary to dart Trish. She'd been driven off by our presence, and I watched her fall in the bush about 100 metres away. Hindsight is a wonderful thing, however, and it was better to be safe than sorry.

By the time Trish was down, Roger had already administered the reversal drug to the calf. I worried about how this tiny baby would now find her family when she awoke. It would be another ten minutes or more before her mother was back on her feet and there was, by now, no sign of any other family members.

Then the most remarkable thing happened. The calf awoke and gave a deep, open-mouthed roar as she attempted to get to her feet. Roger climbed into the backup vehicle which had been trailing us, and moved off towards Trish so that he could inject her with the reversal drug. I was back in my stationary 4x4, standing up through the open roof, with the squealing baby right beside me.

All of a sudden, a young eight-year-old elephant came out of the bush in front of me, running at breakneck speed. Her ears waved as she ran; her body was barely able to keep up with her racing feet. Squealing and roaring, she was heading straight towards my vehicle, and stopped a mere metre away. I knew I was in no danger, and kept my video camera rolling. It was Twilight and she'd come to rescue her baby cousin! Another two T family elephants quickly joined her, all of them trumpeting and roaring, and surrounded the baby. Gently making contact with her trunk, Twilight ushered the de-snared baby off into the bush, with the other two elephants in tow.

'Did you see that?' I later exclaimed excitedly to Roger. 'That was one of the most incredible things I've ever witnessed.' I've never known other animals to look after each other as lovingly as elephants do.

No other jumbos were in the open when Trish came around from the drug, although I felt secure in the knowledge that after she got up she headed off in the same direction that her family had gone.

The next time I saw the T family, mother and daughter were back together, walking happily side-by-side. They were a little wary of my vehicle for a few weeks, but that didn't last for long. The de-snaring had taken place on a Tuesday, and that's what I named Trish's baby.

Tuesday is safe and well and loved by all.

Animal enchantment

Elephants are my first love, which is no surprise to those who know me. When you live in the African bush, though, it isn't long before all sorts of creatures are competing for the title of most endearing. From monkeys to hippos, snakes to scorpions and cheetahs to chimpanzees, I have had the privilege of meeting some extraordinary animals over the years. I've come to adore them all – well, most of them anyway. I must admit to finding some of the smaller critters considerably less enchanting. But it was undoubtedly a special monkey, a noteworthy cheetah and an adorable chimpanzee who first helped cast Africa's magical spell on me.

One of the gentlest animals I've ever known was a wild resident of Hippo Haven in the Savé Valley Conservancy in south-eastern Zimbabwe. He was a regal-looking vervet monkey that was befriended by my friend Karen who still lives in this tranquil spot. She'd named him Boon.

Never given to snatching, Boon liked to raise himself onto his back legs before ever-so-politely accepting a nutritious treat from my hand. I always noticed with pleasure his striking white eyelids as he lowered his gaze, as if out of respect, and tenderly took whatever I had to offer. He was without the nervous hurry of one untrusting. He frequently chose to rest close beside me, sometimes with his hand on mine. With his furry black face and pale bushy brow, he looked like a wise old man clad in a fur coat of soft grey. While sitting cross-legged on the lawn, at one with his troop, I often observed them at play. The youngsters raced around incessantly; bouncing, yelping, squealing and having a ball. I frequently think back to Boon, the gentle one who stole a small piece of my heart.

I'd visited Hippo Haven back in the days when I was not yet ready – not yet game – to give it all up to live in the wilds of Africa full-time. Now I too live among my own troop of rambunctious vervet monkeys. In summer they favour the Zambezi teak trees, and demolish the riot of sweet, purple flowers, which I don't begrudge them at all. I'm less tolerant when they take to the roof of my abode and pull off handfuls of thatch, though. Whenever I hear the thud of agile bodies landing above me I sigh and go outside to reprimand them. I find myself somewhat intimidated by the stares from the males – so unlike how I felt when around Boon – not to mention their large drooping testicles, coloured an exquisite powder-blue.

Although the monkeys stole the show, it was actually a scaled reptile that first welcomed me to Hippo Haven. It rested on top of a thatched roof, basking in the sun. Alarmed, but determined to be brave, I hugged myself calmingly and with an air of indifference that I didn't really feel asked, 'What sort of snake is that?' 'We've got another snake?' Karen questioned casually. She followed my gaze and started to giggle. My fear and loathing of snakes reawakened. I didn't understand her laughter and certainly envied her nonchalance. The snake was short and dark, and sat perfectly still with its head slightly in the air. And it was rubber! It had been placed there in an attempt to deter those mischievous monkeys. I was too relieved to feel stupid. The vervets and I have at least one thing in common: we don't like snakes.

It was at Hippo Haven that my dislike of another blessing of nature came to the fore. I was staying in a quaint little wooden cottage, quite open to the elements. Drying myself off after a steaming shower, I reached for my long black trousers and a sweater, and pulled them on. Karen's home wasn't far away, and before long I set off across the lawn to join her for dinner. The night sky was as spectacular as ever, the silver dust of the Milky Way lighting my path.

It was another glorious night in paradise until I suddenly felt the most excruciating pain on my backside. My hand impulsively shot inside the back of my long trousers and I flung whatever was in there onto the lawn, which was a rather foolhardy thing to do. I was lucky not to have been stung on the hand as well.

Karen came racing out at the sound of my yelps and took on the task of examining the stinging cheek of my buttock. What I'd briefly held in my hand felt scorpion-like and she agreed that a scorpion was the most likely offender, although we couldn't find the little bugger anywhere.

'What colour was it? Was it big or small?' she probed.

I had no idea what colour it was, nor its relative size, but judging by the degree of pain, it surely had to have been big. I was taking no chances. 'It was big,' I declared.

'It's the smaller ones with thin pincers and thick tail that are the most venomous,' Karen responded, trying, in vain, to be comforting.

'Well, it could have been like that,' I mused.

We were hours from any medical help and so, after swallowing a generous helping of antihistamine tablets, there was nothing more we could do but hope for the best.

'How are you feeling?' Karen kept asking. 'Are you nauseous?'

I wasn't nauseous and I didn't have a high temperature, but it's interesting how you imagine symptoms when there's a chance you've been bitten by something lethal and the pain is severe.

Twenty-four hours passed and thankfully nothing happened. I couldn't sit down properly for days, though, and a hard red lump remained for months.

I'd come to Hippo Haven primarily to meet the Turgwe River hippos. Karen knows these animals as individuals and heroically saved them from certain death by hand-feeding them during the severe 1991–92 drought. Before she escorted me out on foot to meet them, she gave me the usual briefing, 'If something unexpected happens, whatever you do, don't run.' I always thought that this must be an impossibly unnatural thing to do. A huge beast is bearing down on you and you're supposed to just stand there?

The setting was serene. A huge crocodile lay outstretched on a bank in the clear water, with a mixture of lush greenery and bare rock all around us. We were walking silently in the direction of a couple of the hippos that Karen knows well, and all of a sudden one was out of the water and charging us. What did we both do? We ran ...

Fortunately, he didn't pursue us for long, but it was an unforgettable, adrenalin-rushing encounter nonetheless. From a safe distance upstream, I anxiously watched him trundle casually back to the water, to resume his otherwise lazy day.

After gathering my composure and catching my breath I gave Karen a side-ways glance. It was evident that this didn't happen to her often and I decided it prudent to bite my tongue. I desperately wanted to ask her if, next time, I should stand still or run! What I also learnt that day, and have since had highlighted to me repeatedly over the years, is that in the African bush it's every man (or woman) for themselves.

I always recall fondly my weeks at Hippo Haven. It had been revitalising to fall asleep to the sounds of a happy chorus of grunting hippos. And I'd fallen in love with Boon. It was certainly a memorable place of the wild, in more ways than one.

*****

There are no hippos resident on the Hwange Estate, where I've spent the past decade working with the Presidential Elephants. I had actually never before encountered one there at all, not even one just passing through. But one day, as I was driving by Mtaka pan, I was astounded by the volume of croaking coming from its depths in the middle of the day and I drove towards the water's edge to take a closer look. The water's surface was completely still, but around its edges there were literally thousands of colourful toads mating. I opened the door of my 4x4 while preparing to take a photograph. I had one foot on the ground when, out of nowhere, a huge hippo exploded from the middle of the pan, mouth open wide, lunging straight towards me. I got the fright of my life, and learnt another lesson: in the African bush you must never assume anything.

My leg safely back inside, I frantically started my 4x4 and backed off a few metres. The hippo retreated from the pan's edge to its centre and started rolling full-circle, all four stumpy feet protruding from the water while momentarily on his back. It was a comical performance, although I couldn't quite work out how he was managing to accomplish this fine feat. He did, however, appear to be mocking me for my rather clumsy retreat.

My thoughts drifted to an earlier trip I'd taken to Mzima Springs in Kenya, East Africa. While on a volunteer bird-ringing expedition in Tsavo West, I visited a remarkable place where the water is crystal clear and a submerged cavern allows you to view the activity of its wild hippos under water. They're certainly more agile than they look. It's quite something to see such enormous mammals appear weightless, as if they're walking and rolling on the surface of the moon.

The behemoth in front of me finished his romp, hippo-paddled to the very edge of the pan and glared at me with nostrils flared. With my heart in my mouth I decided to 'put foot' and get out of there. He was too close for comfort and looked less than amused with me.

Two days later the Mtaka pan hippo was gone, as mysteriously as he had appeared, and I've never seen one on the estate since. 'Where had he come from?' I wondered. 'And where did he go?' It must have been quite some distance and I admired his stamina. I had marvelled at his acrobatic flair too, but was less appreciative of his petulance. I knew, though, that I'd unwittingly encroached on his territory and that he had every right to be cross with me.

* * * * *

Another of the wild places that holds special memories for me is a farm called Elandsvreugde in the southern African country of Namibia. It's home to the Cheetah Conservation Fund (CCF); a place where the magnificent Waterberg Plateau looms large, forming a stunning backdrop. It was here that I met Chewbaaka, an orphaned, hand-raised cheetah who became my friend. As an ambassador for the CCF, Chewbaaka was key in demonstrating to farmers and children alike that humans and these great, spotted cats can live peacefully together.

I spent time with him every day throughout my stay as a volunteer in the late 1990s. I cherished the afternoons when I was able to walk on the open plains with him unrestrained at my side. Like all of his kind, his speed was remarkable and I'd marvel as he completed his regular exercise routine, encouraged to run as he would in the wild.

Back in Chewbaaka's enclosure one morning, I sat down on the bare ground near to his head, yearning for his close presence. He was sprawled out, basking in the sun's warming rays. I reached out and stroked him affectionately. His purring was reminiscent of a jumbo jet and I remember being surprised at the intensity of this incredible sound. Eventually, he got to his feet and shook his lean, spotted body, which seemed to dance in the magic of the African morning. Then he lay back down, closer to me now, and plonked his huge tear-stained face right in the middle of my lap. I was in heaven! Judging by the increased volume of his purring, and the thrilling deep vibrations and dead weight of his head on my lap, so was he.

Everything about Chewbaaka had intensified my love of wild Africa and I wanted to share this small slice of the African continent with others. When my friend Bobby arrived from New Zealand, where I too once lived, to join me, she promptly fell in love with Chewbaaka, and Africa, too.

* * * * *

Bobby had helped me to fill out the application form for my first three-month wildlife-volunteer stint on a remote, uninhabited island named Ngamba – 40 hectares of rainforest in the north-west of Lake Victoria in Uganda, in Africa's east. It was here that I met, and fell in love with, another delightful animal friend – one of the magnificent great apes. While participating as a volunteer research assistant, surveying the vegetation and fauna of Ngamba Island, I had the privilege of meeting an orphaned chimpanzee named Nkumwa, who was less than one year old at the time. She was a victim of the illegal wildlife trade, fortunately rescued, but now living a captive existence in the company of a keeper at the Uganda Wildlife Education Centre in Entebbe on the northern shores of Lake Victoria.

Little Nkumwa had huge amber eyes that bore into my soul as I fed her from a baby's bottle. Gazing at her, with her startlingly familiar facial expressions and hand gestures, it came as no surprise to recall that chimps are our closest animal relative. She held onto my leg – something that she'd learnt to do with her keeper – and walked upright beside me.

The island was converted into an eco-friendly chimpanzee sanctuary the year after our survey of Ngamba was completed. It has become a place where Nkumwa and others of her kind – all of whom suffered great cruelty at the hands of humans and can't be returned to the wild – now live out their lives in a more natural environment. Today, the Ngamba Island Chimpanzee Sanctuary is a popular tourist attraction.

There's scientific evidence that chimps have an appreciation for natural beauty and I often imagine Nkumwa, now 14 years older than when we first met, sitting where I once did on the shore of Ngamba Island watching the sun set, vivid orange, over the calm waters of the lake. I wonder if her thoughts are with the mother she never really knew.

All these years later, my friends and family are still a little perplexed that I gave up an affluent life to live among wild animals in untamed Africa. The sentiments of my close First World friends – a mixture of amusement, bewilderment and awe, along with, they tell me, unbounded respect – are well summed up by this text that Bobby wrote after she'd been with me in Namibia with Chewbaaka, and finally began to understand my choices. Her words offer a little insight into my pre-Africa life; a life that now seems strangely surreal, like it belongs to someone else:

> Sharon was the epitome of the high-flying professional: always immaculately attired, with business jackets and high-heeled shoes; long, curly hair always neatly styled; discreetly made-up; and nails confidently painted in bright, cheerful reds. Here was a woman who wore court shoes to walk her dog! She flew first-class on business trips and stayed in five-star hotels around the world, returning to a harbour-view apartment and a little red sports car …
>
> In 1997 Sharon decided to take some extended time off and indulge

herself in a number of voluntary wildlife conservation missions in Africa. Some promised to be short and comfortable. These seemed reasonable, but her friends weren't sure about her roughing it. She surprised us all by deciding to apply for three months on a tough expedition in Uganda. This was major hardship – no electricity, no generator, no running water, no permanent structures, no chocolate. How would she survive without any of the usual creature comforts?

Friends who better understood the outdoor, camping lifestyle helped her fill out the application forms: Able to create campfire cuisine for large groups? Tick! Yet this was someone who rarely turned on her own stove! Before we knew it she was busily accumulating all of the bits and pieces that she would need to survive: full medical kits, wet-weather gear, sleeping bag, head torch, mosquito net, rabies injections. 'Could she really cope without a hair dryer?' we wondered ...

Sharon said her goodbyes and we wished her Godspeed, quietly wondering if she would survive unscathed. The first postcard arrived after much delay. It was as rough and tough as we had expected, but she was loving every minute of it. She was helping to make a difference. She was home.

As it turned out, I came to realise that I'm at my most content without the usual creature comforts, although it's certainly easier to cope when there's at least the basics of electricity and running water. I haven't had my feet in closed shoes, let alone high-heeled ones, for more than a decade, and I don't think that I ever could again. What's more, I now cringe at the mere thought of an underwire bra!

It's certainly been an astonishing change of lifestyle; a life in the bush, with animals as friends that, despite all of the many and varied challenges, I haven't been able to leave behind.

* * * * *

Not long after I wrote this story, sad news from Namibia reached me. Chewbaaka was dead. He was almost 16 years old and passed away in April 2011 after attempting to bring down a rabid kudu that had leapt into his enclosure. He suffered extensive bruising and tragically didn't recover. The news of his death affected me deeply, as had his noteworthy life. Chewbaaka – king of cheetahs to many – was a legend. He left behind a special and lasting legacy.

The gregarious Ws

One afternoon, the air still with the heat of September, I found myself at Mpofu pan on the Khatshana Tree Lodge-side of the Hwange Estate, which is one of the Presidential Elephants' favourite bars in the bush. I hadn't realised that I was parked right beside one of their new dust-bathing hangouts. The elephants were forever finding new favourite places to churn up the earth.

Wilma, a grand W family matriarch with a large, rounded notch in the bottom of her right ear, walked casually up to my 4x4. She was suddenly only centimetres from my door. Before I could react to her close presence, she picked up a trunkful of red-coloured sand and threw it high above her head. Half of it went over her massive back, while the other half poured in through my open roof all over me.

I cringed, my head, shoulders and arms completely covered in red dirt, and involuntarily burst into laughter. But then I caught sight of my camera equipment on the seat beside me, also coated in a layer of fine dust, and my laughter quickly evaporated into gasps of despair. Wilma didn't appreciate the change in my tone of voice. She looked down on me, clearly a little irritated, her huge head towering above my vehicle and the whites of her eyes visible. I quickly told her how beautiful she was – which usually appeases most females – but all I got in return was another trunkful of red sandy earth. 'You wicked woman,' I mumbled light-heartedly, and quickly got out of there before she tried it again.

There was a mischievous twinkle in Wilma's eye before that second trunk-load of dirt poured in over me. I have no doubt that she was simply having her daily dose of unadulterated fun. I might not always appreciate her sense of humour, but Wilma – grey and grand, wild and wicked – had long ago endeared herself to me forever. It seemed like she was constantly having a laugh, generally at my expense, and knew she could get away with it. Wilma is the size of a tank but as gentle as a butterfly and I love her dearly, bold though she may sometimes be.

Not yet familiar with the antics of the elephants in their new favourite place, I drove just a little further down the road, leaving Wilma to dust-bathe in peace. There were red elephants everywhere. The sun was glistening on their vast backs, their rumbles audible, as they revelled in sloppy reddish mud by the water's edge. Having not yet learnt my lesson I pulled up close beside them, as I always do, and switched off my engine. No sooner had I done this when Whole, a distinguished W family female with a distinctive large hole in her left ear, rapidly thrust her foot forwards and backwards, forwards and backwards, forwards and backwards, kicking up waves of wet, sticky mud that seemed to travel inconceivable distances. Splat. Splat. Splat. *Splat!*

I had mud all over the windscreen, mud on my sunglasses, mud down my arms, mud on my notebooks, mud all over the back seat, mud everywhere. This time I really did laugh, and I imagined the Ws having a good giggle too in their extraordinary, infrasonic, secret language.

* * * * *

Whole is such a mellow giant. In fact I often think of her as a giant marshmallow – all sweet, and soft and gooey inside.

Her teenaged daughter, who has small tusks that curve inward on her trunk, is Whosit. I'm certain that Whosit is confused as to whether her name is Whosit or Stopit, since I'm forever combining these two words when I'm around her. 'Whosit, stop it!' I regularly cry. 'Please, will you stop leaning against my 4x4!'

One day Whosit was pushing down hard on my windscreen, and I was threatening to give her a smack. Some readers probably think 'yeah, right, as if a wild elephant would really do that …' But those who have been out with me and have met the endearing Whosit have no doubt that this really happens. Everyone leaves thoroughly enchanted by her and her incredibly friendly W family relations – all born wild, all living wild and all free to roam wherever they choose, and apparently to do whatever they like to my 4x4.

Whosit is now 15 years old. Our already-close relationship gained intensity after her younger brother, Wholesome, was killed by a neck snare in 2004. Her heartfelt reaction to her brother's death singled her out for me as being a particularly special young elephant.

When Whosit gave birth to her very first calf it was an exciting time. For quite a while, I had no clue if she'd given birth to a girl or a boy. Another elephant in her immediate family, named Whoever because she has no identifiable ear notches and therefore became 'Whoever that is', gave birth during the same week. So there were two babies of exactly the same size, one male and one female, who lovingly shared mothers. Whenever I saw Whosit she had either no baby, or two – one suckling from each breast. Whenever I saw Whoever she also had either no baby, or two – one suckling from each breast! So it took me quite a long time to finally figure out who really belonged to who. As it turned out the baby boy belonged to Whosit and the girl to Whoever. These two little ones, Wish and Wishful, were rarely apart and could easily have been mistaken for twins.

When Wish decided to give my 4x4 a bit of a shake, Wishful was usually nudged up right behind him, her face against his butt, helping to ensure it was a memorable event. The first time they did this I had no idea what was going on. I was looking around at Whosit-height for the culprit but, strangely, could see no one touching my 4x4. When it shook again I looked down, rather than up, and there was little Wish and Wishful just below bonnet level, looking extraordinarily pleased with themselves.

Visitors need not be concerned, though, since they're not so bold with the game-drive vehicles. It is, however, one of the reasons why no private self-drive vehicles are allowed on the estate. All tourists must book a drive on a licensed game-drive vehicle.

Whosit and Wish, and Whoever and Wishful always wander around with grandmother Whole. For years following the untimely death of her young son, the gentle Whole was terribly forlorn. Thankfully, she came into oestrus soon after Wholesome's traumatic death and gave birth to the loveable Winnie in 2006, who rejuvenated her spirit. (Winnie was the name previously given to a calf belonging to the most senior matriarch, Wendy, but both tragically disappeared forever in late 2005.)

Whole heads up a different subfamily from the charming Wilma, but I do frequently encounter them wandering together. They all come enthusiastically when I call to them, promptly appearing at the window of my 4x4. I talk, they rumble; I sing, they sleep; I reprimand, they look the other way. It's a little like a marriage I suppose, but better!

* * * * *

A solo traveller named Lisa asked to spend her days among the Presidential Elephants, with me accompanying her lodge game-drives. I've occasionally, but regrettably not always, been able to accommodate this sort of special request. We all set out together, even earlier than we had the day before, and were lucky to stumble across the Ws around Mtaka pan. They graced us with their implausibly close presence for the next four hours. All of the five W subfamilies were there – Whole's, Wilma's, Wide's, Wanda's and Wiona's. They were awfully keen to hang out with us, just as we were eager to hang out with them.

So enchanted were we, especially with the adorable Whole and Whosit, that we didn't get to munch on our packed lunch until 3.30 p.m., and then it was with endearing jumbos still all around us. 'This is the best day of my life,' Lisa proclaimed. And we both smiled, remembering that she'd declared exactly this the previous day when we'd stumbled upon a different Presidential family – the affable L family with their grand matriarch, Lady – and were privileged to spend extended time with them too. 'Okay then, this is another best day of my life,' she beamed.

* * * * *

Tourists Gertru van Tuyll and her husband Roel turned out to be equally enthusiastic about their time with the Presidential Elephants. Although they're keen birders and naturally fell in love with Hwange's smaller feathered fellows, it turned out that they adored the big leathered ladies too. They asked if I'd jump in their game-drive vehicle one afternoon to see who we could find.

Once again it was Whole and others from the W family who graced us with their incredibly close presence. It was a thrill for Tru and Roel when this sociable family chose to eat grass right beside our vehicle's tyres, which was apparently much tastier when ripped from there.

Tru kept in touch; she became a goodwill ambassador for Hwange and for the Presidential Elephants. She enthusiastically shared her experiences with both friends and magazines, and emailed frequently begging for news about her newfound four-legged friends. I decided that when the day came I would ask Tru to name Whole's next baby. This is an honour, especially when it comes to my favourite elephant ladies, which I don't give out lightly. Tru appreciated the importance of my role as guardian of the Presidential Elephants and was trying to be really helpful. It was the least I could do to say thanks. The Ws were, after all, the reason she'd fallen in love with the Presidential Elephants.

Vervets, leopards, bushbuck and baboons

I t's not easy to imagine it now, but there were days, years in fact, particularly during 2007 and 2008, when the shelves of Zimbabwe's shops were all but bare. Tinned food was impossible to find, as was almost every household essential. As if there wasn't already enough to contend with, we became a nation of hunters and gatherers, with everyone searching for the items they needed, buying more than they really wanted when they found them and then trading with someone who'd done the same and had in their cupboard something that you couldn't find. Word would spread like wildfire that sugar or flour or salt, perhaps, had landed somewhere and crowds gathered like vultures to pick the shelves clean before nightfall. During these times even a simple loaf of bread was a prized commodity.

A young vervet monkey I named Cheeky loved to bound from the open door of my tiny rondavel onto the high partition that separated the bathroom from the living area. The first time I encountered him sitting there I was genuinely startled. He looked just like another of my ornaments until he unexpectedly came to life and walked the length of the partition towards me. I learned that it was best not to madly shoo him away since that caused no end of chaos and commotion. The activity of his troop outside always eventually enticed him back where he belonged. I let him come and go as he pleased for a few months until the day that I wandered inside and found Cheeky sitting on my sofa with a cherished loaf of bread on his lap and the entire middle already demolished.

I shrieked and lunged towards him, unintentionally breaking my vow of tolerance and terrifying him in the process. He scrambled over my coffee table, sending a favourite bowl crashing to the concrete floor, and after that I no longer accepted Cheeky's presence inside. He'd occasionally bound in and out, grabbing a banana or a butternut, until I made certain that nothing edible was ever left sitting in the open.

*****

Vervet sentries frequently sat high in the trees in my garden, raising the alarm whenever danger was near. In this way, Cheeky's troop became my early warning system for snakes, and even once for a leopard.

One day I walked outside to join Last, the mechanic who was working on my aging and unwell 4x4 (he was so named because his mother decided that he'd be the last born), and the vervets were once again in a state of alarm.

'Do you know there's a leopard there?' Last asked casually.

'A leopard where?' I queried.

He pointed to the bush not 20 metres away.

I saw the grand cat lying on the ground, its beautiful coat illuminated by dappled sunlight. There was no movement, though, and suddenly a slight wave of early decay reached my nostrils.

'Is it dead?' I frowned.

'You'd better hope so,' Last uttered straight-faced, watching me walk towards it.

I didn't hope so, but it had become obvious that it was. The young leopard had come close to human settlement only because it was injured and weak. Its body was emaciated. One of its back feet was broken. I see relatively few leopards and a dead one, so close to my hut, was heartbreaking.

I immediately reported the dead leopard to the management of Hwange Safari Lodge, whose grounds I was living on at the time, and asked that the carcass be collected. But this didn't happen. When the Parks Authority personnel arrived the next morning the leopard was nowhere to be seen.

'A hyena must have dragged it off,' they mused, happy to simply leave the situation like that.

'Will you please show me the spoor where a hyena dragged this leopard off,' I demanded indignantly.

There was no animal spoor – that was very clear to me – although there was definitely a lot of human spoor. I was insistent. The police force must now be involved, as taking a leopard, even a dead one, was a criminal offence.

The police eventually arrived. They tracked the human spoor, which matched the shoe print of one of my neighbours, to a freshly dug grave, where they unearthed the skinned remains of the unlucky leopard. They searched the neighbouring houses but the skin was nowhere to be found. Despite the shoe spoor and the skinless remains, no charges were ever laid, which was pretty much the norm at the time.

It was deeply disheartening to know that while some of us tried so hard to protect and save the wildlife, others simply exploited it for their own gain, and got away with it.

* * * * *

I was occasionally able to save a life right where I lived, which made up for some of the disappointments. I awoke early one morning to the sounds of something crying. It was a prolonged, pitiful wail that caused me to wince, and I thought that perhaps something was caught in a snare. I hurriedly pulled on some clothes and raced outside, listening intently. The cry was coming from somewhere behind my rondavel. Something was caught in the wire fence.

In the vacant yard next door, a baby bushbuck, with its delicate, white body spots and white throat patches, had somehow gotten his head through one of the small, diamond-shaped threads in the fence and was unable to free himself. It seemed impossible that he'd gotten himself into this predicament, but having somehow navigated his way into the fenced yard, he clearly couldn't find his way back out.

I raced to him, not sure how to handle this, but knowing there was no one else around to help. The little buck was understandably frightened and he kicked forcefully as I tenderly placed my hands on his body. His hooves were sharp and in an instant the front of my jacket was ripped. Droplets of blood were trickling down his tiny forehead as a result of his struggling and he was so delicate and fragile that I feared hurting him further. I spoke soothingly to him and took off my jacket and wrapped it around him, so that he'd do less harm to himself and to me. I couldn't cover his eyes, though, since his entire face was trapped through the wire.

I had no wire-cutters but somehow, after what seemed like an eternity, I eventually managed to manoeuvre buck and wire enough to pull the little guy free. Keen to avoid those sharp hooves, I held onto his hind legs and, still wrapped in my jacket, I carried him the short distance back to my garden. His little black nose was moist and he had impossibly huge, handsome eyes. He'd calmed down considerably by now and I gently washed the blood from his head. Somewhat reluctantly, after unsuccessfully encouraging him to drink a little water, I put him down on the ground and let him run free. He bounded away without looking back.

I saw him regularly after that, with an adult female close by. They came often to drink from the largest of my birdbaths. I frequently opened my door in the crisp, early mornings when birds chattered incessantly to find the ground in front of me resplendent with tiny hoof prints.

* * * * *

Bushbuck are the only solitary, non-territorial, antelopes in Africa. Although they don't herd together, I often see more than just mother and child together, feeding peacefully, happily sharing their home range with each other, and with the elephants.

Trust was an adult male bushbuck who lived around the Kanondo area. Over time, he became so trusting that he'd pop his head into the open passenger-side door of my 4x4, apparently just to say hello. Sadly, Trust disappeared a few years ago. In his place came a female bushbuck who chose to spend time around the pans in the mid-afternoons. She also became accustomed to my 4x4 and when, a few months later, she turned up with an adorable fawn in tow, I was delighted.

Mother and child often mingled happily with the baboon troop that frequented this same area. In the wet season I watched these playful baboons pick water-lily flowers while manoeuvring awkwardly, making sure they didn't get even the slightest bit wet. Yet in the dry season they'd sometimes immerse themselves completely in the water, with only their cheeky faces protruding from the surface. Then they'd bounce out again quickly and continue their romp around the veld. I nicknamed them the 'Crunchies' given how loudly they crunch the seeds cleverly uncovered from elephant dung. They seemed like such unlikely companions for the gentle, peaceful bushbuck, yet they were often together, the buck secure in the knowledge that the Crunchies would bark loudly at impending danger.

It was only a couple of months later that tragedy struck when the baboons must have been elsewhere. Just the day before, in the middle of the afternoon while on my daily patrols of the land, I'd come across a fat male leopard sitting contentedly on a termite mound. I'd admired his magnificence, observing him for almost an hour. Now I watched the mother bushbuck as she came to drink alone.

Did that leopard …? Oh no, could he have …? It's a harsh reality. Always, there is life and death in the African bush. Always, there are species other than elephants to worry about.

Lady and family

L ady is an unforgettable elephant. She's the first wild elephant who, over time, truly accepted me as having a place in her world, who ultimately consented to my touch and responded with genuine excitement to my presence. This wasn't something that I set out to achieve; it merely happened by chance over the course of several years.

Lady is a Presidential Elephant female that I estimate to be in her late 40s. She is huge and she can be boisterous. She's unquestionably intelligent and powerful in more ways than one. She's wildly entertaining and affectionate to boot. Above all else, she is dignified. The numbers change with births and deaths, and as males become teenagers and leave the family, but right now she is the matriarch of a family of 18. This number will increase by one when the next baby is born, and that's going to be the birth of her own calf.

'Lady!' I squeal. 'You crazy monster! Do you actually want to *drive* my vehicle today?' Her dexterous trunk slithers inside the window of my 4x4 and grabs a hold of the steering wheel. The gaping tip of her trunk worms towards my mouth, exposing two enormous moist nostrils. I'm reminded of a big spongy sea urchin as she exhales a stream of warm air, usually flecked with mud particles, onto my face. She takes my own fingers in the fingers of her trunk and gives me an elephant handshake. Her pull is powerful and I struggle for a moment to release her grip. She concertinas her trunk, like an accordion being played vertically, so that when I rub it, it feels rough and deeply grooved. The flapping of her huge ears is so near that I'm fanned by a cool breeze.

It's mind-boggling that this is a wild, free-roaming elephant. When I arrived on the Hwange Estate in 2001 she was just another elephant.

Once she'd revealed her true self to me, she deserved to be more than this. She deserved to be known.

Lady was the first elephant that I spent extended time introducing to the estate's photographic safari guides. It was late 2005 – almost five years after I'd arrived to work with these elephants – that I began acquainting her with those of the guides that I trusted and believed would act responsibly when she graced them with her exceptionally close presence. It was a responsibility that I didn't take lightly.

Once I'd gained the friendship and trust of a distinguished female it didn't take much encouragement for her and her family to approach other humans. Unlike the guides who drive tourists around on the estate, however, I knew and understood the elephant family hierarchies, their family relationships and other important details. I'd learnt to know the elephants well, both as individuals and as members of close-knit groups, and I'd become expert at reading their moods. I knew that those who didn't properly understand Presidential Elephant behaviour, or who might be tempted to push rules and boundaries in pursuit of a bigger tip, could get themselves and others into a lot of trouble. I wanted the guides to be able to share Lady's splendour with guests, but I was very aware that the delicate balance between familiarity and strife could be fractured in a flash. I'd spent countless hours with Lady and her family and had earned their trust. I knew that if anyone tried to emulate me, without adequate knowledge, they could bring about the serious injury, or death, of a human being, a majestic elephant, or both. And that would be unbearable. It's something that I remain greatly concerned about to this day.

The sheer magnificence of Lady wasn't something that I could keep all to myself, though. I had to trust that the guides, who typically spend only a few minutes with an elephant family before moving on to the next animal, would be responsible and would understand their own limits, especially with so many unfamiliar voices, smells and movements always on-board their vehicles.

I call to Lady, 'Hey Lady girl. Come on Lady. Come here my girl.' And Lady turns and heads towards me, even from hundreds of metres away. Her step quickens, she bounces her head about as she paces towards me and lifts the fingers of her trunk to my hand, much to the bewilderment of the safari guides who, to start with, had to learn how to identify her.

In those days Lady was easily recognisable by her much longer left tusk, combined with the distinctive hole that adorns the middle outer-edge of her left ear. She broke her tusk in 2009 so that suddenly her right tusk was the longer one. Then she broke it again, so that today her tusks are the same size. With time and practice you don't actually need to be able to see her tusks or her ears to know it's her. It's her body shape, her walk, her overall appearance; she becomes as familiar as the friend you meet for coffee.

Lady is frequently splattered in mud, her stunning, long eyelashes caked. As she lumbers my way she swings her tail from side to side, side to side. I don't see any flies and I wonder if elephants waggle their tail in excitement, just like dogs. As she walks by, barely a centimetre or two from my closed door, the entire window is momentarily filled with folds of mud-caked skin, a few larger globules of gooey sludge suspended precariously. I can hear squelching as her skin wobbles in time with her giant steps. She is nothing short of awesome.

In my early years among the Presidential Elephants, when I was still a novice, I actually believed that Lady had twins. This was a mistake I've been careful not to repeat. Females within a family regularly come into oestrus at the same time, and therefore give birth at similar times, often within the same week. Baby elephants, I've learnt, are not opposed to suckling from different mothers. When there are two elephants born to closely related mothers around the same time, the youngsters invariably become great mates and spend much of their time together. They don't seem to mind at all which of the new mothers they suckle from, and frequently suckle from just one of them simultaneously, with one on each teat. And then they switch, to both suckle from the other mother. Such youngsters, just like Wish and Wishful from the W family, can certainly appear as if they're twins. It's only with careful, prolonged observations that you discover what's really going on. Eventually I realised that one of Lady's 'twins' in fact belonged to Lady's sister, Leanne.

Be wary when someone proclaims, 'That elephant has twins!' While twins certainly do occur, they are rare. In more than a decade of tireless observations I've never recorded any genuine sets of twins among the Presidential Elephants.

I think of Lady's family and don't know where best to begin when looking back over their lives. So many tragic things have happened to this family, all of which have affected me deeply. It's difficult to pinpoint which incident distressed me the most. Perhaps it was the disappearance, and likely murder, of Leanne? Or was it Loopy, Lady's son, who we eventually saved from certain death? Or maybe it was Limp, son of Louise, who suffered the most grotesque snare wound I've ever seen. Or it might have been Lee, son of deceased Leanne, who today wanders around with a sliced-off trunk.

Lady's family once had 16 members and at that time a massive quarter of them had been snared. Given how frequently I was encountering this family, combined with where I was coming across them, I knew that they didn't wander far. The culprits were sitting right under our noses; perhaps, I feared, employed by some of the safari lodges whose livelihoods depend on the animals that surround them. In the days before the anti-poaching teams became more vigilant, I have no doubt that the setting of snares by some deceitful employees was one of our biggest tragedies. Today they're no longer getting away with it, at least not to the extent that they once did.

When I last saw Leanne, in September of 2007, she was right beside my 4x4, looking healthy and happy, kicking the ground, loosening clumps of grass and stuffing them into her mouth. As I drove away that day, I told her to help Lady keep the family safe. I sincerely regret not telling her to keep herself safe too, as I usually did every time I saw her. I often wonder if her head is on somebody's wall, or if her impressive, same-sized tusks are sitting, intricately carved, on someone's sideboard. She was almost certainly shot. She disappeared literally overnight. I saw the L family the next day and Leanne was gone. And she was gone forever.

Today Leanne's son, Lee, is ten years old. He was only five years old when his mother disappeared. He and his younger brother Litchis, who wasn't even three when tragedy struck, wandered around by themselves in the weeks that followed her death, distraught and confused. I didn't expect Litchis to survive, but he eventually returned to the security of the family group and has managed to live on. Lee returned too, but just seven months later he fell victim to a vile snare. The end of his trunk was ripped off. This seemed to be the final straw for Lee, as it almost was for me. He was restless and by the time he was just 7 years old, rather than the usual 12–13, he spent increasing amounts of time away from his remaining family. Although he sometimes trailed other Presidential families, I frequently saw him wandering alone. He had become an independent bull before he was a mere eight years old. I felt desperately sorry for him and offered him a tasty acacia pod every time I saw him. I figured he more than deserved it. If his mother had lived, he'd still be with his family today, all these years later.

I'm proud of Lee for how he's coped. His trunk was sliced off in such a way that it's a little longer on the left-hand side than it is on the right. Now with no fingers at its end, he uses his right foot to kick a pod onto the underside of his trunk, which he curls to form a cup. From there he manages admirably to toss the pod into his mouth. He will always be handicapped, though – at the hands of humans. That he has remained so placid is testament to just how forgiving elephants are. They might never forget, but they certainly do forgive. I, on the other hand, cannot find it within myself to be so charitable when atrocities are inflicted on innocent wildlife.

Limp, son of Louise, was horrifically snared when he was just two years old. The wicked loop of wire was so tight around his front left leg that his leg literally burst. It took Limp years to recover. Today he is 12 years old, and his injured leg is not quite as flexible as it would otherwise have been. A faint circle around the lower part of his leg, where the deadly wire once was, is visible even now. Limp still roams with his family. He'll head off on his own soon, though, as nature dictates, to lead the life of a solitary bull. I pray that he'll stay safe.

Loopy, son of Lady, is doing fine after we removed a tight, strangling wire from around his neck when he was four years old. He is now 13 years of age and showing signs of going independent. Lancelot, son of Lesley, was also snared when he was just two years old but fortunately someone – perhaps it was grandmother Lady – managed to pull him free, leaving only a slight leg injury that remained for just a few weeks.

Others in this family are Lucy, Libby, Lantana, Lilly-boy, Laurie, Louie, Lol, Lazarus, Lindsay, Langa and new addition Leopold, all of whom I adore and worry about. As with all of the elephants, I check each of them for snares every time I see them, always desperately hoping that I find no more.

I enjoyed the most spectacular sunset that I've ever set eyes on with Lady and her family. It was also a sound extravaganza. It was Boxing Day 2007. Leanne was dead, but Lee and Litchis were, thankfully, back with the family. I'd spent the afternoon making sure that everyone was okay. Other Presidential families had appeared from the bush and there were more than 50 elephants around me. White-faced ducks whistled their way through tufts of pink and purple cloud. There was the soft rumble of elephants and the soothing gentle popping of champagne frogs (that sound not unlike the tiny bubbles in champagne), in glorious stereophonic sound. Elephant silhouettes were reflected in puddles of rain water now tinted a soft pink. As darkness approached, the bulbous clouds became wispy and blanketed the sky with bands of astonishing deep blue to complement the pinks and purples. Other swollen clouds rolled in like a moving canvas of fluffy marshmallows and took on an exquisite shade of deep pink, lazing just above the horizon before finally enveloping the heavens with belts of burnt orange and burgundy. Egyptian geese honked and red-billed francolins cackled. Elephants slurped and splashed their way through surface water.

Lady stood motionless beside my door, letting out a low, purring rumble every now and again. As night descended I proclaimed aloud to her and my other animal friends, 'You just can't get any better than this.'

A mix of wild and domestic

I've never really understood my unease around horses. Put a carnivorous, black-maned lion or a gigantic, wild elephant right beside me and I'm perfectly at ease. Yet with a horse I see, above all else, huge accusing eyes and whopping big teeth. Although I grew up on a farm in Australia, it was a vegetable farm and there wasn't anywhere close by where I could confront my fear of horses by learning to ride. Years later I watched with envy as my nephews became expert horsemen. As teenage stockmen and rodeo riders they tried to ease my nervousness whenever the opportunity arose, but to no avail.

Even so, this was an opportunity that I wasn't about to pass up: my travelling partner, Gavin, and I were set to ride out on horses in the grounds of a game farm in Harare (Zimbabwe's capital city) to seek out a tiny giraffe born just a few days before. After elephants, giraffes rank as one of my favourite animals. I desperately hoped there was something for me to ride that was akin to a Shetland pony.

Gavin chose a fine horse, confidently swung his leg over its wide, sleek back, and was ready to go. I stood around, kicking the ground, feeling a little forlorn. Rejecting the first horse offered to me, I begged for one just a little more sedate. The handler disappeared for a few minutes and came back with a peculiar-looking mare that appeared to be 200 years old. Climbing aboard – something that I have never managed to do elegantly – I felt a sense of foreboding. This really wasn't a good idea, I thought, but undeterred I smiled the confident smile of the secretly terrified.

As we started towards our goal, I noted with concern that my old mare was stumbling constantly, seemingly unable to lift her front legs high enough off the ground. It was as if they continually buckled beneath her. 'I'm too fat for this horse,' I hollered. Everyone just rolled their eyes, chuckled a little, and told me that she'd be just fine. I needed to enjoy her and move with her. Everything would be okay. At the time I wasn't actually very heavy at all and I took some comfort in the fact that if nothing else, she at least didn't appear to have the stamina to buck me off.

We moseyed along getting fantastically close to zebras, impalas and kudus, which were enjoying the bounty of the green season. The stormy sky was spectacular. Dark, puffy clouds rolled in around us and thunder rumbled. The light rain was soft on my skin and so refreshing after the heat of the day. We were getting close to where the mother giraffe and her baby were known to be resting. If we were quiet, the horses would take us right up to them.

Giraffes are such exquisite animals. Graceful and dignified, they're the runway models of the bush. From up high on the horses, still 25 metres away, the adorable newborn giraffe looked perfectly pocket-sized. An air of excited anticipation was building. The only sound was that of fluid birdsong, and the slow clomping of the horses' hooves on damp ground, as we meandered closer.

I'm still not really sure what happened next. There was this horribly loud shriek – apparently from me – as I was unceremoniously dumped on the ground. Worse still, my right leg was upright in the air with my foot caught in the stirrup! For a few seconds I wasn't sure whether to laugh or cry. Fortunately my foot soon joined its partner on the ground and I sat up, laughing hysterically; my visions of being dragged away happily unfulfilled.

So much for the half-hour that we planned to spend in the company of the giraffe family. They were off at a gallop. I looked up at my old horse. She was gazing down at me coyly, apparently sharing in my bewilderment and embarrassment. I hollered once again with a grin, 'I told you that I was too fat for this horse ...' From that point on I decided that mixing domesticated and wild animals wasn't really for me.

*****

Buddie, though, is more or less a mix of just that. I never imagined that reptiles had much of a personality until I met Buddie. He's a large leopard tortoise that my friend Carol rescued from certain death on Harare Drive. With him, I've savoured peaceful moments.

Although my fear of snakes is legendary, they're actually the only reptile that I don't particularly like. I'm quite fond of the other scaled ones – lizards, skinks, agamas, geckos and monitors. I have no serious aversion to crocodiles and I adore the intriguing ways of chameleons. It's unquestionably the shield reptiles, though, easily recognisable by their characteristic shell, that I like best of all.

The two shield reptiles that I stumble upon most often in the bush are land-dwelling tortoises, which are most often seen in Hwange in the wet season, and fresh-water terrapins. (Turtles are sea-dwelling and so aren't found in the land-locked country of Zimbabwe, as I found out after making that mistake long ago.)

Twelve years ago an African man, who was part of the despicable bush-meat trade, held Buddie out for sale as vehicles whizzed along the busy Harare road. Unable to bear the thought of someone killing and eating this ill-fated animal, and knowing that the authorities wouldn't likely bother arresting the poacher, Carol brought him back to her garden and named him Buddie. He's lived in various large, fenced grounds ever since. I say *he* but I've never been quite sure. Unless you're an expert, sexing a tortoise isn't all that easy. The lower shell is said to be concave in males, and they evidently have a longer tail than females, but when you have nothing to make a comparison with it's not that simple to judge.

Buddie's domed upper shell is 51 centimetres long, with three raised shields down its middle. His small brown eyes are ringed with green snake-like skin; his feet have five long claws and the elongated, overlapping scales on his forelegs look more like fearsome spurs. When he walks, his hind legs take me by surprise, looking like miniature elephant legs. Although he doesn't have any teeth he does have a serrated beak, which, as my fingers can attest, is awfully sharp indeed.

I'm typically only in Harare around Christmas time, and that's when Buddie loves to find me there. His favourite food is in the shops:

plums, peaches, pears, pineapples, apricots, melons and mangoes. He's usually only given the skin and the scraps but he knows that he can get the better of me, and persists until I relent and feed him whole fruits. He doesn't have a taste for strawberries, so I pop these into my festive glass of pink champagne, not feeling obliged to share.

I sit on an outside step in Carol's garden, enjoying the colours and the leafy outlook, listening to the melodious call of the Heuglin's robin and the repetitive kok'ing (kok, kok, kok, kok) of the purple-crested lourie. The grey lourie, or go-away bird, is often around too, telling me with his monotonous cry to do just that. I gaze at a prehistoric-looking hamerkop as it hunts for frogs in the bottom of the nearly empty pool, and at a colourful crested barbet flitting in and around the greenery. Buddie notices me and makes his way right up to my bare feet. If I ignore him he butts me. So I talk to him and massage the soft skin on his back legs which, surprisingly, doesn't make him retract his head. In fact it makes him wheeze happily. And I can't help wondering if he wants to mate with me.

Later in the day, Carol's gardener Fear comes to tell me, 'Buddie's got his trailer with him.'

I look at Fear, puzzled. (He was so named because the hospital he was born in was named Phia – pronounced by his mother in the same way as we pronounce fear.) 'I don't understand what you mean,' I respond.

He points to Buddie, who's walking across the lush green lawn, closely trailed by a tortoise the same brown colour as he, but a fraction of his size. They look like Laurel and Hardy!

The little guy is exactly as long as Buddie is tall – about 18 centimetres. It's a Speke's hinged tortoise. Its shell is much smoother than Buddie's and has two unique moveable joints, one on either side, that allow the tortoise to cover its hind legs and tail when it feels threatened. I try to determine whether this one is male or female, but again I'm easily frustrated. Hinged tortoises don't grow very big and this one is already as long as its kind is said to grow, so I deduce that it's an adult. I rub my hand over its lower shell and feel a slight dip, so maybe it's a male. Its belly is not uniform yellow like a male's is said to be, though, and seems to me to be patterned like a female.

The comparatively tiny tortoise starts to climb on to Buddie, its forefeet resting high on the back of Buddie's shell, its hind feet on the ground. So then, I wonder, is Buddie a female after all, and this other little one a male attracted by pheromones, wanting to mate? Or are they simply enjoying each other's company? I can only postulate, but one thing's for certain, they sure do look amusing.

Just like Buddie, the little hinged tortoise enjoys a meal of fruit, but his diet is even more varied. Unlike Buddie, he enthusiastically chomps into unsuspecting beetles and large, glossy black millipedes (known as *shongololos*) that are sometimes as long as he is. I watch them both, with a renewed respect for shelled reptiles.

* * * * *

I recall the unfortunate terrapin that I once saw meet with a gruesome end. It was the wet season and a crocodile had taken up residence in one of the mineral-lick excavations that are created by the elephants on the Hwange Estate. It held a little water, but only just enough to cover the croc. On the sandy bank behind the crocodile's head were hundreds of bright-yellow butterflies and I pulled up to photograph this curious scene. The croc disappeared on my approach, and when he reappeared I gasped. He had a sizeable terrapin in his jaws. I'd regularly seen this terrapin, or one like it, at the water's edge. I clicked off a few photographs, thinking that this would be over in seconds, but to my horror it seemed to go on forever.

The croc tossed the terrapin around in its jaws; its ample size and hard shell making swallowing impossible. The terrapin extended its neck, its shining eyes were bulging and all four feet were waving in the air. Its shell eventually cracked a little, and then a little more. But it was taking much too long. The terrapin's legs and neck became more and more elongated, and mobile, as the grisly scene unfolded. The croc chomped down harder and harder on the terrified creature, and I was relieved when it was finally over. I knew that the crocodile had to eat; I just wish it had eaten something else.

I'm never particularly happy when an animal gets eaten, no matter what it might be. A few weeks earlier I was monitoring elephants around a pan while at the same time admiring a hamerkop, some African jacanas (also known as lily-trotters) and the resident grey heron at the water's edge. Out of the blue there was a frightful splash. The jacanas and the heron screeched their alarm, a crocodile rolled, and there was no hamerkop in sight. 'Oh, no! Did you really have to do *that*?' I frowned. The assassin swam past with a heavy black bill, a glassy eye and a clump of brown feathers protruding from its jaws …

* * * * *

Carol phoned one morning, as she does regularly to check up on me and to find out how the elephants are faring. Excitement peppered her voice. 'I've just caught the little hinged tortoise with his penis out', she exclaimed, 'and it's huge. He was definitely trying to mate with Buddie.' So I guess Buddie isn't a boy after all.

The changing months
of Hwange

The colours and patterns of the Hwange veld change with each passing month. It's never just the wet or the dry season, unless you're driving around with your eyes half closed. There are so many wonders to enjoy. Every month, of every year, brings something new and different to help relieve the daily stresses. While tourists tend to favour the dry months, when animals in need of water are forced to congregate around the open pan areas, and are therefore easier to spot, I have learnt over the years to love the other months even more.

January is summer in Zimbabwe, a time to revel in the bounty of the wet season. When there's no rain the days are sweltering and the cloud formations in the stormy skies are often spectacular. The trees are in full, dark-green leaf. The grass is lush and tall, swaying gently in the hot breeze. Birdlife abounds, and many migrants are temporarily resident. The crowned cranes, with their striking grey-and-yellow plumage, take turns to nurture their eggs. The stunning reds, oranges and yellows of the flame lilies – Zimbabwe's national flower – are visible, as are other striking wildflowers. The Zambezi teak trees and the hooked-thorn acacias are flowering and splashes of mauve and cream tint the veld. The seasonal pans hold an abundance of water, as do the mineral-lick excavations created by the elephants.

The foamy white nests of tree frogs hang over waterholes. Beautifully patterned butterflies and moths flit among the vegetation, where you might also find a colourful chameleon. Beetles of many varieties patrol the ground, as do leopard tortoises and *shongololos*. It's always thrilling to see these awakened life forms returning after months of hibernation. Babies of all species abound. The impala babies are growing up, as are the young of the blue wildebeest, the Burchell's zebras, the black-backed jackals, the warthogs and the vervet monkeys. Baby waterbuck appear in the veld while the kudus and sable antelope are still heavy with fawn. It's the 'green season' and also a popular birthing time for the elephants. Compared with the dry season, though, sightings are usually few. When the elephants are seen, they're frisky and revitalised, revelling in the surface water and abundant vegetation, with the youngsters racing about playfully.

The days of **February** remain hot. Although rain is still falling the bush begins to take on a less luxuriant look, the lush, green colouring is no longer quite so vibrant. Tall grass bends in the breeze, now a sea of whitecaps as seed heads develop. In the soft early morning and late afternoon light, the green canopies of the *acacia erioloba*s, or camel-thorn trees, appear sprinkled with oversized grey confetti, their countless new seed pods clearly visible. Bright-yellow hibiscus flowers, with dark-maroon centres, dot the roadsides in the early mornings. The water lilies are also coming into bloom, their stunning, large, bluish-mauve flowers attracting troops of chacma baboons.

By now the crowned cranes' eggs have hatched, as have those of the Egyptian geese. The proud parents strut around the veld feeding with their chicks. The babies of the African jacana are growing up too. By mid-February the first of the tiny helmeted guineafowl chicks appear, sometimes in rather staggering numbers. Other birdlife abounds, although by now the many migratory storks are departing. The male shaft-tailed and paradise whydahs (a type of ground-feeding finch) are in full breeding plumage with spectacularly long tails, making for a dazzling display in the sky. Endearing young fawns grace the sable herds, while baby elephants follow close behind their mothers looking like adorable wind-up toys.

March heralds the beginning of autumn, with hot days and cool, crisp early mornings. The tall grass has by now turned into a sea of creamy yellow. In years of good rainfall, surface water is still visible and water lilies continue to bloom spectacularly.

The wary white-faced whistling ducks have had their babies and the new clutches are occasionally visible among the water lilies. The crowned crane chicks are growing up; their budding yellow crowns making them look like little punk-rockers. The young guinea fowl are growing up too, as are the crested-francolin babies, who raise their tails like bantam chickens. Red-billed francolins are sitting on white-speckled eggs. By late March the broods of young Egyptian geese have typically taken to the sky. Kudu babies appear in the veld, joining the sable and waterbuck fawns already born. More newborn elephants, pink behind the ears, scurry to keep up with their mothers.

The days of **April** are still hot, although the nights are now quite chilly. If rain showers have continued to fall, there'll still be some green grass visible among the sea of creamy yellow. Many of the trees are no longer uniform in colour, and differing tones of green are now showing. Sometimes by late April, especially in years of low rainfall, splashes of yellow are visible. The pods are ripening on the *acacia erioloba*s, much to the delight of the elephants who can be seen using their great bulk to shake the trunks of the camel thorns so that their delicious seed pods sprinkle to the ground.

April sees the young of both the crowned cranes and the white-faced whistling ducks taking to the skies. Magpie shrikes, with their long tails, are numerous, and their sweet song echoes around the veld. In some years mopane bees (tiny stingless bees that seek moisture from around human eyes) are already buzzing around incessantly, testing people's patience to the limit.

It is typically a busy month for elephant mating, with celebratory vocalisations echoing around the veld. Cape buffaloes and blue wildebeest are also mating at this time of year, as are the vervet monkeys whose powder-blue and bright-red genitalia signal the male monkeys' sexual maturity. Male kudus, with noses pointed forward and long spiral horns held horizontal along their backs, are also pursuing females on heat. The animals are typically all in good condition, following the past four months of plenty. It's always delightful to see them, now at the end of the bountiful rainy season, with their round butterball bellies.

The days of **May** are normally still hot, but the nights are now cold. The daytime skies are typically clear and cloudless, the night skies resplendent with stars. The grass has mostly dried, sun-bleached to the colour of straw. The thatching grass is tall and ready for harvesting. Much of the surface water has dried up, leaving only baked, cracked ground. The stunning colours of autumn are prominent by now. Trees proudly display brilliant shades of burnt orange, bronze, pink and silver, intermingled with the earlier tones of yellow and green, especially in years of low rainfall. The forests of Zambezi teak are spectacular in the late afternoon light, flaunting their autumn colours. The grass cover is thinning and the reeds in the pans have usually shortened, despite the still relatively low elephant presence.

This is a particularly amorous month. The impalas are rutting, trying to hold on to their territories in the peak of their mating season. Their harsh snorts and grunts echo around the veld. It's also mating season for the warthogs, waterbuck and sable. The male sable, with long sweeping horns, taps his foreleg against the hind legs of a female on heat, a sure sign that he has mating on his mind. A lone female elephant, with only her youngest calf in tow, might be seen alone with the bulls, a sign that she's also ready to mate.

June signals the beginning of the long, dry winter months. The nights and early mornings are cold, the days clear and generally still very warm. Light winds sweep across the plains, drying out everything in their wake. The parched, yellow grass has by now become shorter and thinner. The pods of the hooked-thorn acacias split open to reveal dried seeds, hanging like forgotten Christmas decorations against the clear blue sky. Some deciduous trees are already bare, the veld beginning to take on an unwelcome starkness.

The elephants are shaking the *acacia eriolobas* for the last of the seed pods that they love. With elephant activity increasing, the chacma baboons and the yellow- and red-billed hornbills busy themselves in piles of elephant dung, consuming seeds and anything else edible. Crocodiles warm themselves, basking in the sun on the banks of the pans. Young bushbuck can be seen with their mothers. They're already relatively big, having remained hidden for several months after birth. Roan antelope fawns, with oversized floppy ears but still lacking their black face mask, wander beside their mothers.

Winter heralds a time of fewer bugs – the scorpions, centipedes and spiders around in reduced numbers – and I, for one, am extremely thankful that snakes hibernate! By now surface water is scarce and has to be pumped to the pans in order to sustain the wildlife in this area devoid of dams, rivers and streams. It's time to keep an eye out on the bush roads for discarded acacia stems, with lethal thorns that pierce vehicle tyres. It's also wise to avoid driving over elephant dung, so often littered with these same long spikes.

The harshness of wild Africa is only just emerging, although game viewing is becoming easier with more animals visible around the open pan areas.

In **July** the night-time temperatures may well drop to 10 degrees Celsius below zero (14 degrees Fahrenheit) and the water in garden hoses, birdbaths and 4x4 radiators freezes solid. Night and day temperature variations can be dramatic. Although the nights are prone to frost, the days are usually still pleasantly clear and quite warm. The dense summer vegetation has disappeared, enabling sightings much further into the bare woodlands. Some autumn colouring is still visible, with other bushes standing grey and barren, seemingly lifeless, awaiting the November rains that everyone already hopes won't fail. The grass has turned blonde and brittle. It's difficult to visualise the lushness of January when all now looks so stark, with tones of brown and yellow dominating the landscape.

In the still of the afternoon, trees begin to rustle – a sweeping, whirling sound. Swirls of dry air collect leaves, racing along, touching the ground. These 'dust devils' always manage to unsettle the elephants – perhaps reminding them of helicopters and past culling operations –

and they appear greatly relieved at their passing. Encounters with the beautiful, shy roan antelope are more regular at this time of year. Male bushbuck can be seen taking an interest in the opposite sex, so too the black-backed jackals. Tone-deaf red-billed francolins emit hysterical, raucous cackling at the crack of dawn. Much more pleasant are the frequent night-time calls of both the scops and the pearl-spotted owl.

With the arrival of **August** comes the stark realisation that there are still another three long months before the rains come again. It's dry everywhere. Smoke from distant bushfires, fanned by dry winds, hangs in the air, resulting in spectacular sunsets that colour the sky with shades of brilliant red. The nights are still quite cold, although the days warm up quickly bringing with them the return of those annoying mopane bees.

The naked trees and shrubs give the atmosphere a ghost-like feel, the bare ground littered with elephant dung. Although the ordeal trees tint the landscape with crowns of yellow, and the bottle-green crowns of the evergreen acacias are clearly visible, much of the veld looks drab. It's the harshest time of year for the browsers, with so little leaf left to forage on.

The stunning courtship display of the bateleur – all puffed up, with wings spread, elbows reaching for the sky – is a pleasure to watch, its distinctive cry echoing around the veld. Lily-trotters are busy mating. The now-bare woodlands allow for easy game viewing, with species of all kinds visible. Elephants revel in mud at the edges of pumped pans, emerging as oversized glistening jewels. Rubbing themselves on the houses of termites, they leave these mounds caked with mud. The elephant 'rubbing trees' – velvety smooth trunks covered with this same sludge – are also clearly visible. The elephants dust-bathe more regularly now too, coating themselves with a fine layer of coloured earth – brown, whitish-grey and red. Small bushbuck fawns still follow their mothers, as do the occasional Cape buffalo newborns, but few other babies are around. The endangered painted hunting dogs might be spotted, though, with puppies that have recently left their den.

September heralds the beginning of spring, when plants burst miraculously into new life. There's a welcome splash of lime-green, yellow, white, pink and red in the veld. It's a time of optimism, some trees flowering profusely, others flushed with dazzling new leaf – the colours reminiscent of a spectacular autumn – in the silent hope that the rains will eventually arrive to sustain them. It's a remarkable phenomenon of the vegetation reviving itself in anticipation of the rains, rather than as a result of them. For right now the land remains dry and thirsty, the days hot and hazy. Typically, there's been no rain of note for the past six months. The *acacia erioloba*s are prominent in the veld, their crowns charmingly cloaked with miniature balls of bright yellow for just a few weeks. The combretums are flowering profusely too, their greenish-yellow and white blossoms on leafless stems attracting colourful sunbirds. The msasa and munondo woodlands flaunt alluring shades of pink and crimson, while the forests of Zambezi teak are still typically grey and bare.

Smoke from bushfires, often still raging, combine with the incessant dust to dull the sky. The reward is spectacular sunsets. Game viewing is reaching its peak, but for the wildlife it's a harsh time of year. Bare patches scar the ground, surrounded by tufts of sun-scorched grass bereft of nutrients. Kudus, bushbuck and giraffes are fortunate to be able to nibble on the long-awaited fresh, spring leaf. With no permanent sources of water, it's imperative now to pump water for the wildlife. Elephant families arrive at the pans to cool their bodies. The little ones lie down in the shade of trees to rest on their sides, whiling away the heat of the day. Cape buffalo herds, hundreds strong, come to quench their thirst, and are tailed by hungry lions.

Around the pumped pans, the bird life is becoming more lively. A grey heron pair might be building a nest of twigs, while a pair of stunning saddlebill storks wanders about energetically. The colourful lilac-breasted rollers are mating, and their rolling courtship displays in the sky are mesmerising. The masked weavers are starting to breed, the males now sporting a bright-yellow body and black face mask. They're visible in colonies on the acacias, skilfully weaving their basket-like nests, which is a sign that the rains are close. But there's also less pleasing news for me. The snakes are once again active, occasionally seen slithering across the road ahead. Spiders too are more obviously about.

The veld now holds its breath for rain.

October is 'suicide month'. It's a term used in these parts to describe the depths of despair that one can sink to while in the grip of the unrelenting October heat. Temperatures often soar above 40 degrees Celsius (104 degrees Fahrenheit) day after day; the heavy thick air makes it difficult to take a deep breath. The shimmering heat is tangible and waves of thick, black dust roll down the vlei, carried by dry winds, creating the illusion of smoke. Dust devils swirl in the parched veld under a blazing sun. There's a savagery in the air. The veld is thirsty. Bushfires continue to rage.

By late October there's turbulence of a different kind in the skies. Clouds build up mockingly; savage, spectacular electrical storms boom and flash across the sky; the promise of life-giving rain is more often than not only an illusion. Everyone longs for a soaking downpour.

Cicadas (also known as Christmas beetles, despite them looking more like over-grown flies) emerge, their monotonous, shrill vibrations sometimes ear-piercing as the males attempt to attract a mate. The tiny stingless mopane bees are around in force, driving everyone to distraction. Mosquitoes buzz annoyingly, like tiny kamikazes on their deadly approach. Soon, plenty of other bugs will join them.

Those who visit only at this time of year often leave with the mistaken belief that the African veld is perpetually grim, drab and hostile, looking unlikely to ever recover. But flourish it will, as it always does, when the rain begins to fall. By December the terrible harshness of October will be forgotten – until next year.

Violet-backed starlings arrive, adding a splash of iridescent purple to the veld, matching the rich shade of the deep-purple bougainvillea. The African golden oriole adds a touch of brilliant yellow, the Klaas's cuckoo an exquisite dash of metallic green, while the stunning African paradise-flycatchers once again sing their lively song; the male's long tail-streamer is a delight. You might see large flocks of Burchell's sandgrouse around pumped pans, saturating their breast feathers, cleverly carrying water back for their chicks to drink.

Game viewing is at its peak, with animal species of all kinds congregating around pumped pans, desperate to quench their thirst. Elephants move lethargically, avoiding the midday heat by resting under trees with young, fresh leaves. Those elephant babies conceived in the wet season of two years ago are now materialising. Red eyes and bright-pink colouring behind the ears are good indicators of those less than two weeks old. The Burchell's zebras are heavy with fawn, and the impala ladies are also moving with bulging bellies. Warthog and tsessebe babies appear. So too the vervet monkey babies, and black-backed jackal pups in dens by the roadsides. Cape buffaloes and elephants emerge from the bush in their hundreds while lions and painted hunting dogs patrol the veld, taking advantage of weary prey. Dull eyes convey the harshness of what these herbivores are enduring. The ground is all but bare, the grass cover at its most sparse, and the wait for good rain goes on.

Rain sometimes falls by **November** and there's once again lush, green grass for the wildlife to feast on, enabling them to regain condition lost during the long, seven-month dry. But when no rain of significance falls during late October and early November, the veld remains desperate for moisture, and the wildlife is in dire need of greater sustenance. Violent thunder storms disturb the otherwise calm nights, teasing with the promise of heavy downpours but too often delivering only a light shower.

Three little miracles occur without fail following the first generous shower of rain, which does eventually arrive. Firstly, large swarms of flying ants emerge in the early evenings. Fluttering in the sky, these young termites promptly shed their wings and start mating, on a frantic mission to establish new colonies. Then, within a few days, bright-red fireball lilies appear in the veld, their large ball of blazing scarlet on a single green stalk always a striking sight. And then, as if by magic, there's a faint suggestion of greenness on the ground.

Extraordinary numbers of summer visitors appear. Dragonflies are in the air everywhere, like miniature aircraft hovering in the sky, mating after the first showers. Countless frogs and toads mate too, croaking relentlessly. Crocodiles, monitor lizards and fish-eating birds feast on them around the pans. Dung beetles appear, rolling their balls of elephant droppings, in which they lay their eggs. The wingless *toktokkie* beetles, tapping their abdomens on the ground in an effort to attract a mate, emerge and the large nocturnal rhino beetles, together with scores of *shongololos*, are also about. Tortoises suddenly materialise too. Flocks of European swallows and Eurasian swifts, hundreds strong, manoeuvre in the sky, skimming the surface of pans in order to drink and bathe. Flocks of colourful European bee-eaters do the same, twittering loudly in the sky. The stunning lilac-breasted rollers can be seen discreetly breeding in holes in tree trunks. Striped cuckoos appear, as do the black variety, calling their monotonous cry for rain. By now the red-chested cuckoo has also arrived, his loud, relentless, 'quid pro quo' call driving everyone to distraction. The Egyptian geese are mating and the territorial scuffles between pairs are clearly audible. Knob-billed ducks arrive too, the bill of the male adorned with an enlarged fleshy protrusion, signalling his readiness to mate. More elephant babies are born, although the elephant families tend to 'disappear' with the first rain – perhaps following some sort of migratory instinct – making sightings less frequent.

The remaining naked trees start to come into leaf in another brief, brilliant display of autumn-like colouring, despite the fact that it is spring. Spectacular new-leaf tones of green, coppery red and bronze temporarily tint the veld. November brings with it the fervent hope that steady rain will fall for the next four months.

December heralds the beginning of summer, bringing very welcome rain. The veld is instantly transformed. Soaking rain replaces the often violent storms of late October and November. The longed-for changes are rapid and wondrous, the metamorphosis spectacular. Bare, sandy soil is replaced by lush, green grass, the trees and shrubs suddenly, once again, in full green leaf. Surface water sits where dust devils recently swirled and mushrooms push their way through the sand.

Masakhe, son of Misty

Hanging out with the Presidential Elephants on the Hwange Estate

Nkumwa

Boon and friend

Chewbaaka

Andy and Lol on Fraser Island

The shaft of bright light, the day after Andy's funeral

Greeting Lady

There are elephants everywhere when I look out of my 4x4 window

Enjoying a sundowner at Mpofu pan

Lady's gooey trunk slithers in through the side window of my 4x4

Whole, with a distinctive hole in her right ear

Will-be, daughter of Whole, with older sister Winnie

Misty, mother of Masakhe, ripped her right ear in 2010

With an entire pan at their disposal, the Presidential Elephants choose to bathe right beside me

Dusty mineral-lick excavations are transformed into small pans, and are now home to crocodiles. It's nothing short of miraculous. The veld is reborn.

The monotonous shrill call of cicadas reverberates around the veld. The night skies are dotted with the tiny lights of fireflies. Brightly coloured butterflies with quivering wings sit on the damp sand. The large and beautiful citrus swallowtail is known as the 'Christmas butterfly', given its prevalence at this time of year. In some years the African migrant, a smaller butterfly, light-lemon coloured with a tinge of pale green, abounds, resembling a mass of delicate snowflakes in the sky. It's a time of celebration; a time of renewed hope.

Wildflowers once again bloom in the bush, luxuriantly defying the seemingly infertile Kalahari sand. Early in December the smell of wild jasmine fills the air, delicate white flowers dotting the fields of green. The sickle bush (known locally as the 'Kalahari Christmas tree') is bejewelled with small, pendulous two-tone yellow and mauve-pink flowers; they are stunning Christmas decorations to behold. The spectacular yellow, orange and red wavy petals of the flame lilies curl backwards to form striking spheres of three-tone colour, usually by mid-month, another indicator that Christmas is close. Attractive mauve flowers start to bloom on the Zambezi teak trees.

Impalas have their babies early in the month, crèches of these vulnerable fawns visible in the veld. Blue wildebeest and Burchell's zebra foals also frolic on gangly legs, while warthog piglets scamper behind their mothers. Herds of majestic elands are occasionally about, also with babies in tow. Banded mongooses engage in social chatter, their young cute and comical. Although born at any time throughout the year, juvenile giraffes are seen more frequently. Elusive elephant families revel in the lush, green conditions, playful now and re-energised.

By late in December there are Egyptian geese babies waddling behind their parents. Pairs of beautiful crowned cranes feed in the veld, preparing to have their babies. They can also be seen among the reeds of the pans, preparing their nesting sites. Flocks of white and Abdim's storks, hundreds strong, sometimes soar high in the summer thermals.

The resident marabou storks are joined by scores of others; the many migratory birds that arrived during October and November are still about.

When it's not raining the days and nights are hot. Rainy days bring welcome relief from the heat, but they also bring with them less-welcome scorpions, centipedes, snakes and spiders. If you think a Kalahari Ferrari might be your sporty game-drive transport, think again. It's a speedy, really rather scary, eight-legged solifuge – a spider-like creature with beady eyes that can grow as big as your spread hand.

The cycle of life in the veld repeats itself over and over again. It's never all peaches and cream but it is indeed a privilege to be able to observe the multitude of wonders that the changing months bring, always revealing something a little different every year.

An alien way of life

It was at the height of the land invasions and the unethical hunting that negatively affected the Hwange Estate in the early 2000s, during Zimbabwe's land-reform period, that I felt in desperate need of a break from the constant battles. I was tired of all of the threats and intimidation, as people tried to get rid of my eyes and ears in the field. Carol and some other friends whisked me away to The Hide luxury safari camp for a few nights of rest and healing. It's on the other side of Hwange National Park, where Andy is buried. With all that was gravely affecting the wildlife around me at this time, my dreams had turned dark and disturbing, yet at this peaceful tourist camp I enjoyed a pleasant, peculiar dream, vivid as mine rarely are.

I was a passenger in an open game-drive vehicle. We hit a bump and I went sailing up into the air, higher and higher, while the vehicle continued on its way. My friends quickly realised that I was no longer in the vehicle with them and they looked around frantically trying to find me. There I was, floating high in the sky, strangely suspended in the cool air above. They reversed at speed to try and catch me before I plummeted to earth. I didn't plunge to the ground, however. Instead, I sailed gently back down through the clear air and landed, unharmed, precisely where I'd been seated beforehand.

I awoke in a fit of uncontrollable laughter. Fearing that I'd wake my two girlfriends who were sharing the tent with me, I buried my head beneath my pillow. For some reason, though, I couldn't stop the laughter that was so intense it left me gasping for breath.

Early the next morning I told my friends about the dream. As it turned out I had in fact woken them during the night, but they'd left me alone because they thought that I was sobbing and needed to rid myself of all the tragedy surrounding me at that time. They were both awfully relieved to hear that it was actually laughter that had awoken them.

We lazed on our beds, analysing my dream and speculating about its meaning. We finally concluded that I was on a bumpy journey, experiencing things totally alien to a normal way of life, but everything would be okay in the end.

I'm still not sure why I reacted with such laughter, but the dream had given me a strange sense of comfort. It's a comfort that I often think back on, and not only when there are really trying times in the field.

Years later I'm still on this same bumpy journey, frequently experiencing things foreign to a 'normal' way of life. There are always so many challenges, both large and small, to deal with. Sometimes the little things can be the greatest source of frustration – little things as tedious as tiny ants.

Millions of ants climbing up the drainpipe and into the concrete tray of my shower was one thing, but sharing my bed with them was unquestionably another matter. It used to happen more times than I like to recall.

For almost a decade I slept on a piece of foam, a broken piece at that, on a cement floor. Every evening I pulled the foam out from the seat of my sofa and made up my bed, unfurling a mosquito net over it all. There were nights of power rationing when everything was pitch black, and I was jumping and jerking about at 2 a.m., tangled in the net, slapping arms and legs and other places, doing the get-these-goddamn-ants-off-me twist.

At these times I could wholly relate to P. J. O'Rourke, who wrote:

There are ants in numbers large enough to confuse the people who calculate national debt. There are ants all over every leaf and stem (not to mention every shoe and sock), ants all over the ground and around all the tree trunks, and ants climbing in droves up the jungle vines. Which is something they don't tell you in the Tarzan books: He went ahhEEEahhEEEahhEEEahhEEEahh as he swung through the jungle because he had ants in his loincloth.[1]

---

1 O'Rourke, P. J. *All the Trouble in the World*, Pan Macmillan, Australia, 1994.

There were ants in numbers large enough to confuse those who successfully tallied their Zimbabwe one-trillion-dollar notes. There were ants all over sheets and pillowcases, ants in your hair and ants in your undies. Ants in the African bush could literally be a pain in the butt.

* * * * *

Power rationing is another inconvenience I've learned to cope with. In Zimbabwe, candles aren't something you light for ambience. In the cupboard – or in my case, in a cardboard box – there's always dozens of them, ready for the inevitable power cuts that occur daily in the cities and, thankfully, far less frequently in the bush. Candles are always on hand, except when they too were difficult to get hold of and it was necessary to find something desirable enough to trade for someone else's endangered stick of wax.

I've always taken pleasure in collecting different types of grasses; there's an incredible variety to be found in the bush. I particularly like those stalks that are tinged purple and retain their mauve colouring when dry. Both candles and dried grass frequently spring from empty bottles of Amarula (South Africa's heavenly equivalent of Baileys) on top of my small fridge, the eye-catching elephant label exuding a comforting warmth.

I'd been enjoying a glass of Amarula one evening when the lights went out. With the glass tinkling with ice in one hand, I fumbled around with my other trying to locate a box of matches. After finding one I placed my glass on top of the fridge and struck a match. I'm sure I actually struck the usual three or four, since Zimbabwean matches invariably seem to be on their own private mission to frustrate. I guess I'd moved the bottles while cleaning and, with a whoosh, candle, and grass, were alight.

'Holy shit!' I cried, and without thinking picked up the glass from in front of me and threw its contents onto the flames. That was not smart. It was, after all, *alcoholic* Amarula! I realised what I'd done while the smooth velvety liquid was still in mid-flight. 'Shit, shit, shit …'

The small square blanket that I used in the field to keep dust from my camera equipment was just an arm's length away and everything was quickly under control. I had been foolish. And I was lucky. I lived under bug-infested, highly flammable, thatch.

*****

There have been numerous other days in the Hwange bush when I've found myself simply *feeling* foolish.

One such time was after I sighted an elephant calf with a snare around her neck. I was awfully relieved to see that this shameful loop of twisted wire wasn't yet too tight. I phoned for darting assistance despite believing that I wouldn't get help on this day, since all of those qualified to dart were known to be elsewhere. I left urgent messages regardless.

Thankful that the wire was not yet slicing this young elephant's throat, and having convinced myself that the required help wouldn't arrive, I decided to drive further afield in an attempt to track the movement of other elephant families – three of which were also afflicted with deadly wire snares at this time.

A messenger reached me, on foot, with news that one of the darters had altered his plans and was on his way. He'd already been to take a quick look at the neck-snared elephant and had gone to collect darting equipment and rifle support. He'd left a man high in a tree, keeping an eye on the movement of the elephant family.

I raced to find them. More than two hours had passed since I had seen the snared one, so I knew these elephants would no longer be where I'd left them.

Phones at the time were totally unreliable; vervet monkeys had pulled handfuls of thatch from the roof of my hut; there was no fuel; my 4x4 wasn't starting when the engine was hot, which threatened to leave me stranded in the bush; and here I was hurrying along rough, dusty roads *looking for a man in a tree*. 'Only in Africa,' I whispered out loud to myself with a shake of my head.

The whole state of affairs left me feeling more peculiar than ever, and I couldn't help but wonder, yet again, what on earth I was doing here.

* * * *

Despite the challenges of this strange sort of existence, laughter always helps to lighten the mood.

Bantering around an African braai is always fun, and when you're joined by a steady stream of playful elephants, slurping and rumbling around a floodlit waterhole, the atmosphere becomes even more jovial.

The chef on duty stood behind the red-hot coals of our night-time braai, with a giant bowl of meat positioned beside his sizzling grill.

'How would you like your steak?' he asked me politely.

'Only a small piece thanks. I don't eat very much red meat. And well done please, I like mine dead,' I grinned.

There was a series of chuckles, followed by silence. Then from beside me came mutterings in isiNdebele from a white-skinned man, followed closely by a few more black-skinned chuckles. I turned to the white man and smiled, asking him to translate what he'd just said. 'Not dead for me,' he'd requested. 'I'll have mine just a little bit hurt!'

And so we parted company, he with an apparently delicious medium-rare slab of beef on his piled-up plate and me with my miniature piece, which did actually look more than a little bit hurt.

Later that evening I sat with an assortment of white Zimbabweans and foreign tourists for after-dinner drinks. Long luxurious campfire flames licked the cool air as young elephants splashed and played in the nearby pan. The tourists stared contentedly into the fire, listening to, but often not comprehending, the unfamiliar words that frequently dominated the conversation. It was the likes of *laaity* (child), *flattie* (crocodile), *hunna-hunna* (problem), *lekker* (nice), *katundu* (luggage), *dopping* (drinking alcohol), *muti* (medicine), *nyama* (meat), *babalas* (hangover), *dagga* (marijuana), *hondo* (war) and *fundi* (expert) that baffled them. After ten years I still couldn't mask the smile that this mixture of slang and local languages always brings, although I now feel quite at home with the formerly alien banter.

White Zimbabweans have actually become alien beings themselves. These days the saying goes that you're more likely to see an elephant in Zimbabwe than a white person. Given the numbers, that's probably quite true. I certainly encounter far more elephants than I do white people.

'Wanted'
(dead or alive?)

Many love the *idea* of living in untamed Africa. It's actually living here permanently, though, as opposed to visiting, that can frequently get your blood boiling.

I knew that something unbelievably preposterous would eventually happen, since the year to date had been relatively uneventful. Despite the beauty and the fun times, absurd events had, in actual fact, been the yearly norm for me since my 2001 arrival in the Hwange bush. This particular incident happened in 2008, and by then I was becoming quite accustomed to the ridiculous.

There's an expression, from bygone days, that has repeatedly rolled around in my mind since my arrival in Africa: 'Beyond this place there be dragons'. It's what the early map-makers declared when they believed that they'd arrived at the edge of the world, and it seems to sum up my life in the Hwange bush where something unsavoury always appears to be lurking just around the corner, ready to pounce.

This particular year spewed forth a grand measure of the outrageous. In April I found myself on the wanted-persons list of the Zimbabwe Republic Police. I remember feeling rather like Ned Kelly. I had visions of my mugshot being hastily printed on a sheet of paper, along with a reward for my capture.

In reality, my name was fourth from the bottom on a list of names displayed in a glass-fronted cabinet outside the public entrance to the police station in the small rural township of Dete. I was listed among those wanted for poaching, breaking and entering, theft, assault, fraud and rape. No doubt there'd been a murderer or two on prior lists.

Beside my name was the trumped-up charge against me: 'Disorderly conduct'. This was just another round in a long list of intimidation attempts, which first began when land claims commenced in these wildlife areas in 2003.

It's true that I'd used a disparaging word. As a derogatory term for women, the word 'bitch' is said to date back to the 14th or 15th century. It's routinely defined in dictionaries as a slang term for a woman who is spiteful, unreasonable, aggressive or overbearing. There was a woman who worked for the largest hotel in the area, where I once lived, whose mission in life seemed to be to frustrate my volunteer work as much as possible. Over many years, for what I considered to be valid reasons, I'd come to consider her to be a spiteful, unreasonable, aggressive *and* overbearing woman.

During one period of heightened provocation I'd used the aforementioned word to describe her in a casual email of complaint to her higher management that I'd trusted would be handled with discretion. Forever attempting to make life as difficult for me as possible, she was now refusing to sell me petrol even though it was readily available for sale to others. This meant that I couldn't carry out the daily monitoring of the estate and the elephants that I'd been doing unfailingly for years.

It wasn't the first time that this had happened. Having been regularly involved in uncovering deadly wire snares set close to this lodge's staff compound, and having once successfully initiated a trap to catch an employee red-handed with a poached impala, I was never going to be their favourite person.

With friends in high places, and clear encouragement from others with somewhat dubious agendas, she managed to get hold of my email and filed a formal charge against me for using the 'b' word. This was inexplicable enough, but why on earth was I now on the wanted-persons list?

I could only shake my head, astounded, pondering why I hadn't yet been arrested. I was white-skinned, fair-haired, with rimless glasses over blue-green eyes and the only female matching this description at the time for at least 200 kilometres. I lived a mere 20 kilometres from the police station in a sparsely populated district. I drove an easily recognisable 4x4 in an area where there weren't many vehicles on the roads. I spent my days with the elephants, but was home every evening by nightfall. And the police couldn't find me! What's more, no messages had ever been left for me. If the local police force were that incompetent, why would I do their work for them and drive to them? After six long, crazy months had passed, and I heard that the word on the street was that I'd be 'locked up if I didn't turn myself in', I drove into Dete to speak to the officer in charge (since moved on elsewhere) and his staff.

My situation was apparently amusing to them, although I didn't share in their humour. They were demanding that I either pay a fine or go to court. There was little interest in my side of the story, which again was evidently humorous. No one could even explain to me how the charge against me equated to 'disorderly conduct', or what exactly the fine that they were demanding was for. After nearly an hour of fruitless talk, I decided that they could go ahead and subpoena me and that I'd see the relevant parties in court.

I climbed back into my 4x4 and drove away wondering, as I'd done before, just what sort of country I'd chosen to live in. I heard nothing more and another six long months passed. Nothing happens in a hurry in rural Zimbabwe. My name, I was told by friends who passed by the police station, remained on the wanted-persons list. I continued with my elephant monitoring, taking strength from my unique animal friendships, but this was an unsettling shadow that hung over my wildlife conservation efforts.

*****

During this period I often fell asleep to the whirr of a tape from a memorable seminar that I'd attended in 2000 with my IT colleagues. It was a Michael Carrick relaxation tape.[2] I'd lie in bed listening to the tape, trying to put my day to rest, attempting to let go of all of

2   Carrick, Michael. *Journey to The Middle Kingdom: Relaxation with Michael Carrick*, The Carrick Group, 2000.

the hurt and pain and nonsensical behaviour that I'd experienced and encouraging my body to rest and relax. It was meant to be a journey into dreamland, and it unfolded something like this:

A soothing voice flows from the tape deck, encouraging you to take a look at all of your achievements and successes, the gifts that you've given to other people in your life and all of the gifts that have been given to you.

Then, with birds chirping softly in the background, you imagine yourself in a rainforest – somewhere just for you. As you begin to walk slowly through the forest, you notice the trees, the flowers and the birds. You're totally alone, totally at ease. You become aware of a flowing creek and you walk towards the sound of that creek.

Leaning against a towering tree beside the creek, you feel the strength and the warmth of the tree trunk on your back. You notice that large leaves are floating down the creek, drifting by you, sailing around a bend and out of sight.

You're encouraged to place all of your sadness, worry, anxiety and hurt on these leaves as they float past, allowing them to drift away on the current of the creek. You smile at your own courage and wisdom for letting go of things in your life that you don't need. You continue to place one item after another on the large leaves as they drift by you, allowing them to disappear around the bend.

Finally you notice a very large golden leaf and you know that there's one more nagging thing that you really should let go of and allow to drift away around the bend ...

But often times it just didn't work for me. Those who *really* got under my skin kept falling off those damn leaves and swimming back to shore to torment me some more! I often awoke, feeling as if I hadn't slept at all.

* * * * *

Eventually, in April 2009, more than 12 months after this saga first began, my friend Shaynie and I drove in her small car to the Dete police station. Shaynie had seen me through many preposterous times over the years, not the least of which was in 2006 when I'd been formally accused by a government official of being a spy working for the Australian government, assigned to frustrate Zimbabwe's land-reform program! Over time, and after some undisguised threats on my life, it became clear that the unscrupulous harassed only those they feared. Insignificant others were left in peace. Evidently, I was doing my job really well, but it was all so very tiresome just the same. Shaynie and I had just enjoyed a weekend of wildlife inside Hwange National Park, savouring peaceful braais and star-filled night skies, and her supportive presence was comforting. She'd convinced me that I needed to find out if I was still on the wanted-persons list, as many were saying was still the case. Aware that they could well throw me in jail if I was, I tucked my hair under a cap, kept my sunglasses on and ensured that I had a reputable lawyer's phone number in my bag. The camera on Shaynie's mobile phone was ready for action, so long as she managed to stop shaking long enough to take the photograph that I was after. We were both uneasy but I wanted proof of this ongoing saga.

With a glance at each other and a nod of our heads in solidarity, we opened our car doors outside the Dete police station and walked together towards the display cabinet. Shaynie reached up and nervously ran her finger down the list. There was my name, with the charge against me, still clearly legible on the piece of A4 paper. But a horizontal line had been neatly drawn through the middle of it.

Shaynie clicked off a photograph while I pondered yet again what on earth I was doing here.

Misty and Masakhe

Misty, identifiable by two small pieces of skin that dangle from her right ear, is not an ordinary elephant. More than anything she loves to be close. I don't actually remember the very first time that I encountered her. As was the case with all of the Hwange Estate jumbos back in 2001, she was merely a member of a relaxed family, who showed no particular interest in me or in anyone else. I allocated the letter M to her family and went about giving all of her relations names beginning with this letter, for ease of identification.

We choose our friends based on traits that we like and respect, and we find ourselves attracted to some people more than others. There are those we opt to spend time with, a few who brighten our world, but not everybody is the sort of person that we want to hang out with. To my initial surprise, I found that it was exactly the same when it came to me and the elephants. They all have different personalities, just as we do. As I spent ever-increasing amounts of time among the family groups, I found myself more attracted to some jumbos than to others. There are pretty elephants and those not especially attractive, there are those who make you laugh, those who always appear happy and others that you sense are sad. There are those who are born leaders, others who are playful and cheeky, some that are much more talkative than their family members and still others who are incredibly gentle, polite, resourceful and distinguished. (I've never met an arrogant, overbearing, self-absorbed elephant, but I can't say the same when it comes to the human species I'm afraid.)

Misty was gentle and polite. She was a pretty elephant with unusually small ears, sad eyes, and a dignified aura. I was drawn to her. Once named, I'd stop whenever I spotted her and I would sit and observe. There's no off-road driving on the estate, so she'd have to come to me, if that's what she chose to do, rather than the other way around. I talked to her, sang to her and just hung out with her. Over time, she came closer and closer to my 4x4.

I named the matriarch in her family Mertle. I was drawn to Mertle too, but the reasons for this were more complicated. She had spunk. She was huge and deserved respect. She was a leader and took no nonsense from anyone. I liked her immediately.

Misty and Mertle both became my special friends and were closer to me than other members of their family who I also came to know well. In time, Misty allowed me to rest my hand on her trunk, often very close to her eyes. There have been hundreds of times when I could have reached out and touched Mertle, but somehow it hasn't seemed appropriate. She likes to have the upper hand and I respect that.

It's not about being able to touch them, however, or being the first human to form such a close relationship with each of them, as incredible as this may be. This has never been my goal. It's about the intimacy of two different species simply choosing to spend time together and how extraordinary this is in itself. Misty will sometimes stay for more than an hour, right beside the door of my 4x4. She clearly relishes the closeness and the familiarity, just as I do. She rumbles – a thrilling sound when it's so close at hand – and I try desperately to understand what she might be saying, either to me or to her family members. Playfully, I sift through the possibilities:

'It's scorching hot standing here under the harsh African sun. Won't you please move under that tree?' which I won't for fear of falling snakes.

'That's the worst singing I've ever heard, but like any good friend I'll stay to be supportive.' She's a very tolerant girl when it comes to my limited vocal abilities.

'I really should wander down and fill my belly with water,' and I encourage her to do just that, but it's always as if she thinks she might miss out on something riveting if she leaves my side.

Older males wander by and give us a sideways glance. When it's clear she's answering someone else's rumble, I imagine her conversation being with one of these males:

'Misty! What are you doing over there? You really must stop acting as if you're human.'

'Oh Maverick, won't you please be quiet. It's just us girls catching up on some gossip.'

I lean out of my window and give her trunk an extra lengthy massage, and tell her about my week. We're both where we choose to be.

When Misty gave birth in October 2008 she had her young calf Merlin, who was one month away from being four years old, by her side. Merlin had been the light of Misty's life after she tragically lost her previous elephant child in November 2002 to unknown causes. I was thrilled to come across her new, tiny, bright life when it was just a few days old. It was another boy! Misty brought her newborn son right up to the door of my 4x4. He stumbled alongside his mother, his eyes bright red, his ears still flat against his head.

'Hello little guy,' I said to him, beaming. 'Welcome to this world. What's your name going to be I wonder?' The sight of him filled me with a deep warmth and an increased motivation to keep carrying on my work with the Presidential Elephants.

I decided to give Shaynie the honour of naming him. He was a special little elephant and she'd already enjoyed some very memorable close encounters with his mother. I knew that she would do him justice by coming up with a great name.

By now Zimbabwe had pretty much hit rock bottom. Shaynie's life savings, like those of countless others, were worth absolutely nothing. Her pension plan was worthless too. There was no food to buy, and no money to buy it with anyway. For a while it seemed like there was no future in this country, and no hope.

I've never forgotten the day, not long before Misty's baby was born, when I was in a gift shop in downtown Bulawayo, the shelves all but bare. The few customers wandering around were white. A young mother, probably a tourist, with a spluttering baby on her hip, turned to a much older lady and asked politely, 'Do you happen to have a tissue?' The irritated response reflected all too well just what sort of sorry state Zimbabwe was in at the time. 'A tissue? Do you know how much a tissue costs in this country?'

The elderly lady shook her head incredulously and walked away. She may have been rather rude but she was right. Nobody bought boxes, let alone small packets, of tissues, even if you were lucky enough to find them, since they were an imported item and outrageously expensive. I dug into my handbag and handed over a wad of scratchy green toilet paper; it was not exactly what anyone could call 'tissue', but it was the only alternative available at the time.

Everything in Zimbabwe was broken. Nobody even had a tissue to spare.

Shaynie turned to the poetic isiNdebele language for a name for Misty's baby, one that had real meaning in the current day. People were sharing the little bit they had. Two teaspoons of sugar in the coffee of a visitor, not knowing when or if it could be replaced, was a sacrifice no one resented. All hope was not gone and people were rebuilding. Many had no choice but to try.

Shaynie chose the name *Masakhe*, which means 'to build' or 'to rebuild that which has been broken'. She knew that for me, and for the Presidential Elephants, it was also a fitting name. So many things had been broken for us too, and it was time to try to rebuild.

The next time I came across Misty I leaned out of my 4x4 window and, gently placing my hand on the head of her baby, I christened him Masakhe.

Pans and more
of the preposterous

There was plenty of renewed interest in the Presidential Elephants after the South African release of *The Elephants and I* in March 2009, and I realised that there were still two things that I sought to accomplish. I wanted to get the pans on the Hwange estate scooped, after years of neglect, to improve their water-holding capacity. And then, once there was adequate dry-season water for my thirsty pachyderm friends and all of the other wildlife, I wanted to actively encourage more tourists to return to Hwange, to experience the magnificence of these unique elephants. Nothing in Zimbabwe is ever as simple as it sounds, however.

At this time African Sun, the large corporate company who leased and ran the Hwange Safari Lodge, claimed to have sole responsibility for the largest portion of the estate where the Presidential Elephants roam. For years I'd watched the gradual degradation of this land. The distressed wildlife was ultimately forced to move elsewhere every dry season to find adequate water in order to survive. In 2009, encounters with the Presidential Elephants were still too few and far between for me to promote tourism here, as had been the case for the past five years.

My attempts to scoop some of the estate's key waterholes actually began a few years earlier, in 2005. This was a dreadful drought year and even Kanondo – the only pan remaining on this section of land that usually held a little dry-season water – was cracked and dry, with such a slight depression that it was never going to hold good water, even when the rains came. When African Sun declined to act, I arranged for the loan of equipment from the nearby Painted Dog Conservation Project, but their small scoop turned out to be inadequate. We did manage, though, somewhat laboriously, to deepen just the outer edges of Kanondo pan, so that it immediately held more water than it had previously.

I'd been fighting the misinformed for years. 'Just let the pans be. You'll break the seal,' they cried. Various people mysteriously claimed that the use of a bulldozer would break the natural seal of the pans, so that they wouldn't hold any water. I could see no logic in such a claim if the work was done properly and besides, what did it matter? The pans hadn't held any water, or only insufficient amounts, for years anyway. What difference would it make if we broke the so-called seal? But the deluded stayed vocal, and critical. Even after the successful deepening of the outer edges of Kanondo pan, they weren't changing their tune. It became increasingly clear to me that this was nothing more than an excuse for continuing to do nothing.

The year after using the Painted Dog Conservation Project equipment, I was still trying to do something more. I secured a generous offer that would allow us to make use of the heavy equipment being used to build a nearby dam. All it would take was the cost of the fuel to transport, and run, this equipment for the duration of the job. Exasperatingly, even this charitable offer went begging.

By 2009 I was tired of badgering those who clearly couldn't be bothered to act, even at little cost to themselves. The water situation on the estate was as desperate as ever, and the elephants and other wildlife continued to suffer. It was heartbreaking to see the land in such a degraded state. I was determined to arrange for the proper scooping of these pans myself, before there was no wildlife left around to concern myself with. The local Ndebele people have a saying, *'Ithendele elihle ngelikhala ligijima'*, which means 'don't just sit there bleating, get up and do something about it!' I had tried before. Now I simply wouldn't take no for an answer.

At the time Shaynie worked in Bulawayo for a company called JR Goddard Contracting. Through her, I'd met and mingled with other

Goddard employees, some of whom had become friends. I knew that this company had the equipment for the job, but I had access to very little money. The most I could persuade African Sun to part with was a mere US$1,400 towards a job – which they were actually wholly responsible for – that would typically cost in the vicinity of US$20,000. I could raise no more than another couple of thousand from donor organisations. I'd given up trying to raise money to cover my own annual fuel expenses, so many people thought it odd indeed that I would try to raise money to help out African Sun, who had always done so little for the Presidential Elephants. As this was privately owned and leased land, everyone knew that the responsibility lay with the landowner/ lessee. Despite this major obstacle, it took only a few emails between me and Jim Goddard for genuine interest and enthusiasm to be ignited – interest and enthusiasm for my work, and for these elephants.

Jim is a softly spoken third-generation Zimbabwean, as great in kindness as he is in stature. He arrived at Hwange Safari Lodge, with his brother Tom, to meet with me. We drove out onto the estate, surveying dry, cracked sites, like antbears deciding where to burrow. I could feel the enthusiasm mounting amid the discovery of small, dry wallows, created by the elephants in past wet seasons. In addition to the scooping of this land's three major pans – one of which hadn't held any water at all for five years, another that hadn't held any dry-season water for the same length of time – it would take just a few extra hours of dozer time, and more goodwill from Jim, to ensure that some of these mini-pans also held greater quantities of rainwater.

On our way along the sandy road to Kanondo, to agree what could be done there, came a gift from above. The great matriarch Lady, leading the L family, appeared on the road ahead. Forever awed by the nobility of these wild, free-roaming giants, I called loudly through cupped hands, 'Lady. Lady girl. Come on Lady. Come here my girl.' Mighty trunks swung rhythmically as the entire family lumbered our way. It wasn't long before Lady held my hand within the fingers of her trunk, and fluttered long, elegant eyelashes at the Goddard brothers.

It was a thrilling, especially close, encounter, and so fitting that the grand Lady, of all of the Presidential Elephants, would come to introduce herself. It was the icing on the cake that sealed the incredibly generous scooping deal with Jim. After five years of so much futile talk, it had taken me only five days to secure genuine interest, and it would take less than five weeks to plan and complete the entire job.

The dozer equipment arrived on a long flat-bed truck, just a few weeks after Jim's initial visit, and I spent my days from dawn to dusk with Tom, overseeing every minute of the scooping process. Tom transported fuel from Hwange town and we talked endlessly, and occasionally squabbled, about how each pan should best be scooped.

'We need to remember that all of the wildlife, including the giraffes, must be able to drink with ease. We need gently-sloping sides, on three sides at least,' I insisted multiple times every day.

Tom whistled loudly over the din of the dozer to secure the driver's attention and I'd lift my arm and motion in the air for a more gentle curvature. We needed depth, but I was also insistent that there be no sharp-edged or steep sides.

There was a small amount of water in Kanondo pan at this time, which meant that we couldn't scoop it. Given that it was the only water on the land, we couldn't let this pan dry out, since that would have left the wildlife with no water at all. So we agreed that we would create a separate, but connected, pan at Kanondo.

Mtaka pan was relatively simple. We just had to carefully avoid creating those too-steep sides.

Mpofu pan was the one that hadn't held any water at all for the past five years – not even rain water in the wet season. Tom and I watched worriedly as the dozer brought out scoop after scoop of pure sand. But it had once held good water; I knew that for certain. There had to be a clay base there somewhere. And there was, eventually, but there was still an awful lot of sand. So we decided to also scoop a smaller, alternate, pan higher up in a pure-clay area, just in case.

The scooping of these three key pans, and another three smaller ones, went off without a hitch. There was no breaking of any seals. There was no negative effect whatsoever.

My left eye turned out to be the only casualty of this momentous endeavour. The days were awfully hot, glary and dusty. Every day by sundown we were bone-weary and grubby, rubbing our irritated eyes. It was during the course of the third day that something other than sand blew into my eye. It became blood red and felt as if it had been sprinkled with glass fragments. For months afterwards it flared up constantly. I finally made a trip to Bulawayo to see an ophthalmologist, who removed what he identified as a minuscule piece of plastic from the surface of my eyeball.

We had scooped the pans in time to take advantage of the 2009 rains, which began in October. Thankfully, it was a generous wet season. They filled to their brims and the wildlife returned. The smaller pan that we'd created at Mpofu, just in case, was swallowed up by the large body of water that now sat there. Elephants once again rolled and splashed in the new expanses of water at Kanondo and Mtaka. The scooping was a smashing success.

I remember fondly the day that I transported both the bulldozer operator and the low-bed truck driver through Kanondo in my 4x4. The grand elephant named Wilma appeared at the tree line and, when called, lumbered straight to my door. Neither African man had ever seen an elephant in the wild before, let alone one responding in this way. Looking at me sideways, the low-bed truck driver whispered with a half grin, 'Arrhhh, but now I am scared of you. You have very special magic.' From then on he always bowed his head and patted his heart whenever he saw me, not realising that it was in fact these elephants, rather than me, that possessed special magic.

An elephant named Lucky, one of Lady's family, gave birth not long before the scooping began, and I came upon her and her tiny baby one afternoon by the roadside. Lucky brought her newborn right up to the door of my 4x4. I gave Jim Goddard the honour of naming this special little elephant, and he called her *Langelihle*, or Lunga for short, which is an isiNdebele word meaning 'good day'. And a good day it was.

Until I prompted the African Sun management, I didn't receive any thanks for resurrecting these waterholes, and at such little cost to them. As hoteliers they didn't seem to understand the tremendous value of this having been done. When a thank you did finally come from the Harare-based management, it was two short sentences in an email.

* * * * *

It was just after the completion of the pan scooping that the preposterous event of 2009 occurred. Those dragons were back yet again! The fact that it occurred didn't surprise me – nothing surprised me anymore – although I certainly was shocked and disheartened.

Sport-hunting trophies of all shapes and sizes suddenly adorned the walls, floor and shelf surfaces of every public area inside the Hwange Safari Lodge. This was a *photographic* safari lodge, or at least it was supposed to be. It had been through so much with unscrupulous land claims and unethical sport-hunting in areas just a stone's throw away. I'd campaigned hard, with support from others, to get the hunting banned and the land returned. Now this lodge suddenly looked like a hunting lodge itself.

There'd always been a huge elephant head in the guest lounge. In 2005, after land claims and sport-hunting had negatively impacted the Hwange Estate, the higher management had actually considered taking it down, but it was only one trophy. It was particularly large and not one that I had any appreciation for, but at least it was just one. Now, there were mounts of dead animals and dead birds everywhere. This went against the ongoing work of so many conservationists in the area, and I certainly wasn't the only one offended by it, although I was undoubtedly the most outspoken.

I offered my wildlife photographs (of high enough quality to be accepted by magazines around the world) for enlargement at no charge, as alternate décor, but this proposal was rejected.

Complaints from the general public flooded in and the media ran negative stories. I'd just scooped the surrounding pans in order to help *save* the wildlife and yet here we were, surrounded by a horde of dead animals. Heads of animals even appeared behind the tour desk. Many wondered what it was that this lodge was now selling – photographic safaris or hunting safaris? Yet the management continued to assert that they were receiving nothing but positive feedback and declined to even consider removing the heads. Actually, they weren't just heads. A massive half-buffalo stood in front of the check-in desk, taking up an imposing portion of this space and glowering at those who came to the area to enjoy the *live* wildlife.

It was three long months, with repeated pleas that finally had to be escalated to CEO level, before the menagerie of hunting trophies was removed, and sanity finally restored.

It was another win for the wildlife.

Sharing the splendour

He introduced himself as Terry. He'd arrived from South Africa bearing thoughtful gifts of chocolate, wine and sweet-chilli sauce. There was also my favourite Amarula, made with the sweet fruit of the marula tree so loved by elephants. In fact there were two bottles of this delectable liquid wonder. I liked him already.

In the still warmth of a Hwange winter's day, we ventured out together on a game-drive vehicle. He'd requested my company at the time of making his lodge booking, in the hope of some special encounters and more in-depth stories and background about the Presidential Elephants and their close-knit families, and I'd been able to oblige.

We were parked in Acacia Grove, a cathedral of towering trees on the Hwange Estate, and I'd just called to Eileen and her offspring Eumundi, Eketahuna and Echo. Suddenly from the seat behind me, I heard just one elongated word, 'Shhhhiiiit!' I glanced around at this generously proportioned middle-aged man, trying to judge the tone of his muted outburst. Perhaps it was, 'Shhhhiiiit, these elephants are actually responding to their names!' But then again, maybe it was more like, 'Shhhhiiiit, these elephants are now coming straight for us!'

Whatever it was, he wriggled his rump around but soon started to relax, clicking away with his camera. He was visibly taken aback. So long as I remained vigilant, with these well-known E family pachyderms so near, there was nothing to fear, although Terry clearly wasn't so confident just yet.

There are two things that I always stay alert to whenever the elephants are so close: their eyes and their subtle body language.

I've never seen a more beautiful eye than that of a relaxed, free-roaming elephant. When the sunlight hits it just so, it takes on the colour of the ocean. Beautiful, as only Mother Nature is capable of. Sitting so near and gazing up through their implausibly long eyelashes, you feel as if you could swim, and drown, within the depths of their eyes. It does, however, take on a completely different look when the elephant is ill at ease. As for body language, I keep a close eye on the tilt of the head, the curvature of the ears and the positioning of the tail. And the legs – when the back ones are crossed, as they so often are around me, you know you're beside one particularly relaxed jumbo.

Less than a metre away from us Eileen crossed her back legs and dozed, in pure pachyderm pleasure.

I've known Eileen's tuskless daughter, Echo, since she was just a youngster. With a distinctive hole in the top, outer edge of her left ear, she's currently the only tuskless elephant in the extended E family (numbering more than 30), which is an odd thing. I don't know who her father is, since in macho male style, all male elephants mate and then disappear, although I assume there's a tuskless gene somewhere within his natal family. He would not be tuskless himself, though, since I've never encountered a tuskless male in Hwange.

Echo was pregnant for the very first time. This was evidenced by her growing breasts which, unlike those of humans, only develop during the course of the first pregnancy. Soon, I knew, Eketahuna and Eumundi would have a niece or nephew to fuss over.

Eileen's immediate family all have names that remind me of a happy past. My friend, Eileen, lives in New Zealand, where Eketahuna is the name of a small rural town; and we visited the Eumundi markets in Australia, on Queensland's Sunshine Coast; so Eileen, Eketahuna and Eumundi became E family elephants. Echo is a little different. Her name comes from an elephant in Amboseli National Park in Kenya, immortalised by the BBC documentary, *Echo of the Elephants*. They are all special elephants, with special names.

'What's your best memory?' I asked Terry at the end of his stay. He'd met and mingled with quite a few different Presidential families, with some unforgettable encounters, yet he didn't need time to think. 'That very first encounter,' he said, 'with Eileen and her offspring.'

It was the first time he had gazed into the mesmerising eye of one of Hwange's Presidential Elephants.

* * * * *

Inspiration regularly flows in from South Africa. A text message from a man unknown to me read, 'Her heart is still in Africa'. He was messaging me on behalf of his sister who had made a kind contribution towards my fuel expenses. It was odd, I suppose, that she'd chosen to move from Africa to Australia, while I'd chosen to do the opposite. Those six words, 'her heart is still in Africa', played over and over in my mind.

Africa is many things to me, but the most special of these are embodied in the elephants. It's the way golden sunlight glints off ivory tusks; it's the earthy smell of fresh dung; it's elephants of all sizes revelling in dust, mud and precious water; it's the extraordinary contrasts between the wet and the dry seasons; it's those long elephantine shadows at last light; it's their haunting rumbles amid vivid sunset colours and massive silhouettes wandering gracefully under silvery moonlight. These are the special occasions that, once experienced, always remain in one's heart. It's these sorts of memorable times that cause citizens and tourists alike to leave behind a small piece of their heart in wild Africa.

* * * * *

It was July and it had been an unusually quiet time in the field. Some days are just like that, with few animals visible in the open. In the middle of the afternoon I hopped on a game-drive vehicle with international guests and for the first two hours there were few sightings. The gentle Misty and her family came to our rescue for sundowners in Acacia Grove and that made up for everything. They stayed close by while we savoured a cool drink and the privilege of peering into their remarkable family lives.

We left them, reluctantly, to drive along the vlei back home. It would be dark in less than half an hour. Not far down this bush road we encountered a huge rhino bull, a little further on two lionesses, then a herd of buffalo and then – could it actually get any better – a leopard by the roadside! The Big Five in just 30 minutes. Now that's pretty incredible.

Another group of tourists left their heart behind in wild Africa that day.

* * * * *

Smaller things are just as special to me. Every year, around late July/ early August, colourful toads in their thousands awake for just a day or two to fill the air with booming song and to mate. Usually only vocal and visible in the wet season, it is an extraordinary spectacle to hear and see so many of them around the pans in the middle of the dry season. Then suddenly, once again, all is quiet.

There's always *something* to look out for, no matter what time of year it is, like manketti nuts in elephant dung. One afternoon I collected 95 manketti nuts from a huge pile of elephant dung at Kanondo. The bull that deposited this monstrous heap was apparently a nut-loving elephant! It's a shame that he didn't gain any real benefit from eating these. They are the fruit of the manketti tree, which favours Kalahari sand. Their hard, woody shell ensures that they remain untouched by the elephants' digestive system. And they taste really good as the key ingredient in 'manketti-nut cake', despite having been collected from a pile of pachyderm poo.

Such a cake is really delicious. You'll have to trust me about this.

* * * * *

Over the past decade I've occasionally been a guest of the rustic Sikumi Tree Lodge, nestled at the end of the Hwange Estate vlei. On this particular full-moon occasion, the camp was packed with French, Italians, English, Americans and Zimbabweans.

A guest named Belinda had also flown in from South Africa to spend just three days among the Presidential Elephants. Perhaps it sounds like a long way to come for just a three-day break, but these elephants are worth it. Most memorable for Belinda was the unexpected, overwhelming tears of emotion that she had never before experienced while on holiday, despite having travelled far and wide. They struck when she departed from Sikumi, having to now leave behind her new-found elephant friends …

The grand matriarch, Lady, and her family were the first elephants to make an appearance. It was two nights before full moon and Lesley and her son Lily-boy (I had incorrectly sexed the calf as a girl and had to alter the name accordingly) remained suckling by the roadside as we drew near with safari guide Zebedee behind the wheel. Other youngsters approached us merrily as I called out loudly into the night, 'Lady. Lady girl. Come on girl.'

I knew that Lady, as Lesley's mother, had to be somewhere; even adult females are never far from their mothers. Eventually Lady appeared out of the moonlit darkness, trunk swinging rhythmically as she hurried our way. It is always magical to have wild elephants so close under moonlight, with their warming rumbles, and the pleasing sounds of grass being ripped from the earth.

As well as Lady, Lesley and Lily-boy, there was Lantana (Lady's youngest), Libby (Lady's cheekiest), Louise and baby Louie, Limp, Lancelot, Lucky, Lol (soon to be first-time mother) and more. It had been Belinda's only elephant encounter on that game-drive, but it had definitely been worth the wait.

When the Es appeared in daylight the next afternoon it was another memorable time and we spent hours alone with the elephants. As always, it was Eileen with offspring Echo, Eketahuna and Eumundi who stole the show. Matriarch Emily graciously allowed them centre stage. With more than 40 elephants surrounding us under an umbrella of towering acacias it was both thrilling and humbling.

The next day the W family left a lasting impression. With only tips of flapping ears visible, a group of elephants rested beneath shady trees a few hundred metres away. Binoculars couldn't help me identify who this group was. But the Ws were on my mind and with a distant glimpse of familiar body shapes I took a chance and shouted into the wind, 'Whole girl. Come on girl. Come on Whole. Hey Whole.'

It was actually Willa who led the brisk procession of more than 50 elephants who were all now jogging towards us. (You think elephants don't jog? Well, it wasn't exactly a run, but it was definitely not a walk!) All of my favourites were there: Whole, Winnie, Whosit, Wish, Wishful, Whoever, Willa, Wilma, Worry, Wasabi … an awe-inspiring extended family. We stayed with them – or was it the other way around? – for hours during the mid-afternoon.

We'd watched, with a glass of wine in hand, the simultaneous setting of the sun and rising of the full moon. We'd seen wild dog, cheetah and all of the Big Five. We'd listened to the fiery-necked nightjar sing his song while sitting wrapped in blankets beneath the gleaming Southern Cross and nearby tail of Scorpio. This nightjar supposedly sings 'Good Lord, deliver us'. Deliver us from *this*? No way! We'd enjoyed campfires and bush lunches and dinners. Everything was so special. The unique Presidential Elephants of Zimbabwe, however, proved once again to be *most* special. I'm biased I know, but tourists are not.

'I'll be back,' Belinda whispered through tears.

Little did I know that jealousies associated with me helping to give tourists a memorable experience would eventually cause me more trouble than I could imagine. It would become another battle; one that impacted eager tourists.

The thrill of
the unexpected

My early Australian childhood embedded a deep affinity for the wild in me. I learnt early in my life to pay attention to the many natural wonders surrounding me, both large and small, and I understood the importance of protecting them.

I feel fortunate to have been born and raised in Australia. It's legendary for being home to the unusual, and its animals certainly are just that. Its kangaroos and wallabies bounce around, with their young maturing in the warmth of a furry pouch, while the adorable koalas don't do much more than eat and snooze. The platypus and echidna are strange mammals that lay eggs, while the delightful wombat lives underground, and who could forget the legendary dingo or the peculiar Tasmanian devil. As for the birds, the emus can't fly and colourful cockatoos, parrots and parakeets live in great flocks in trees rather than in cages and there's a giant kingfisher aptly named the laughing kookaburra.

Then there's Australia's aboriginals, who are renowned for their memorable music produced from a didgeridoo – a word that sounds just as wonderful as the strange and captivating sound that it makes. Billabong and boomerang always roll off the tongue very nicely too. Perhaps it was talk of the evocative term 'The Dreamtime' – that part of aboriginal culture which explains the origins and traditions of the land and its people – that turned me into a bit of a dreamer. The wide open spaces and relaxed lifestyle makes for friendly neighbours, who are always ready to greet you with an easy-going 'G'day'. Even with the heat, dust and flies it's a magical place for a little girl to grow up in. Yet it's wild Africa that has surprised me most with the thrill of the unexpected.

Before his premature death, Andy, his wife Lol and I shared some unforgettable adventures. I have especially fond memories of a rhino relocation, which didn't go quite as expected. It went perfectly well for the rhino I suppose; it just didn't go quite so well for me.

Andy, who was in charge of the operation, granted me permission to stand close by, alone at the base of an acacia tree, so that I could photograph the release of this particular radio-collared rhino. Andy was also a pilot and was already up in the helicopter, all set to monitor where the rhino wandered. His men were on the ground preparing to release this great horned creature.

I knew that when the door of the transportation crate was opened, the rhino would be free to run off in any direction. I watched him back out slowly and for a few moments he moved only his head, taking in his new surroundings. I stood admiring his ancient splendour, wondering how anyone could slaughter such a magnificent beast for its horn. Then, as luck would have it, the rhino turned and charged straight towards me. 'Oh, give me a break,' I remember thinking. 'You could have run in *any* direction.'

I wasn't about to miss this opportunity though. I snapped a photograph of him in mid-stride, thundering straight towards me. Then I found myself scrambling for my life up the acacia tree. Long, sharp, white thorns ripped my arms before I managed to reach a safe height.

Trying desperately to keep hold of my camera – I wasn't about to lose that photograph now – I gazed down from my precarious position to the rhino below, his huge horn not far beneath my feet. 'Don't move. Don't move,' somebody yelled at me, while everyone looked on helplessly. Don't move? Where on earth could I possibly move to? I knew to be still, so as not to attract any further unwanted attention.

Luckily for me, but not so luckily for them, a group of spectators momentarily grabbed the rhino's attention. After scattering them, he disappeared into the bush and I was soon free to climb down from the tree, a little shaken and nursing my bleeding 'rhino scars', which I was secretly rather proud of a few days later. Standing once again at its base, with two of Andy's men making certain that I was okay, I looked up into the tree and wondered how on earth I'd actually got up there. I was glad that I didn't have to do it again, since I wasn't sure that I could.

Andy eventually landed the helicopter, blissfully unaware of the commotion on the ground, and signalled for Lol and me to jump in, the chopper's blades still whirring loudly in the still of the African morning. As we flew back to his Umtshibi base I couldn't help but ponder, with a shake of my head, what comparatively routine things my friends and family were likely to be doing Down Under. They would have had a fit had they known I'd just been chased up an acacia tree by a rhinoceros!

✳ ✳ ✳ ✳ ✳

When you spend your days in the African bush you learn to expect the unexpected. A slender cheetah could step out of the bush at any moment, on the hunt for dinner; a goshawk might swoop down before your eyes to grab a slithering snake with its talons; there might be a majestic leopard with her cub lazing in the last light on a termite mound just ahead or perhaps a male African jacana cleverly carrying tiny babies beneath his wings. Then there's those times when the unexpected takes you by complete surprise.

Whenever I see a buffalo herd I find myself fighting an overwhelming urge to get out of my 4x4, wave my arms in the air and yell 'shooooo'. There's a scene in the movie *Out of Africa*, starring Robert Redford and Meryl Streep, where Redford does just that and the buffaloes obligingly retreat. I've undeniably watched this movie far too many times.

It was New Year's Eve and I'd popped a bottle of bubbly into my cooler bag before driving out to spend my afternoon among the elephants. By 5 p.m. I was feeling decidedly relaxed. A herd of over 200 buffaloes was making its way up the vlei and, although feeling particularly playful, I once again successfully fought off the urge to try out Redford's performance. Then something odd caught my eye and

I did a double take. It wasn't Rudolf the red-nosed reindeer (running a tad late) in the lead, but it could well have been a distant cousin, perhaps Brenda the blush-nosed buffalo?

Instead of the normal black, like head and body, her broad shiny nose was bright *pink*. It did indeed almost glow. With deformed horns growing downwards, she was a strangely handsome bovine specimen, leading her followers through the festive season. I had seen lighter pigment on the noses of buffaloes before, but never anything this extraordinarily bright.

Arriving at a termite mound on her way to water, Madam Blush-nose paused momentarily, bowing her head. There was obviously a hole in the mound that I couldn't see because four warthogs, perhaps shocked by the sight of her bright-pink nose, shot out of that mound in a flash, startling us all.

The buffalo herd quickly regrouped and moved on to quench their thirst. While they were still at the pan, a tawny lioness, who'd evidently been trailing the herd, wandered over to the termite mound and sprawled herself languidly along it. There was no sign of the lively warthog family and for that I was grateful. They probably owed their life to the buffalo with the bright-pink nose.

* * * * *

Buffaloes always remind me of John – my old-timer Zimbabwean friend who now lives in South Africa – who was once seriously gored by one. When with John you certainly had to expect the unexpected. We shared in the tragedy of Andy's death and later in memorable adventures that sometimes involved buffaloes, but more usually involved horribly huge and hairy spiders.

I won't ever forget the day that I was screeching frantically into the telephone with John on the other end.

'Where are you?' John demanded. 'What are you doing?'

'I'm at home. I'm standing on my sofa,' I blurted.

'Oh.' I could hear the resignation in John's voice. 'Okay, so you'd better tell me why you're standing on your sofa.'

Doom is a brand of insect-killing spray and I always had plenty on hand, much to John's dismay. The night before, I'd sprung off this same sofa when a massive baboon spider ventured out from beneath it. I'd *Doom*ed the poor creature until it was literally covered in a thick layer of white, foamy liquid. They always make such horrid popping sounds when squashed, and I couldn't bring myself to whack him with my footwear. So I laid a tissue over the top of him and left him to expire.

In the morning I wandered over and tentatively removed the tissue, satisfied to see a dead spider with legs all curled inwards, and then sat down on the sofa. Out of the corner of my eye, a few minutes later, I caught sight of movement. Its legs were in motion. It was coming back to life! Who was this creature that half a can of *Doom* couldn't kill? I raced again for the can, gave it a good shake and pressed down hard on the nozzle. 'John, get your butt over here and look at this spider for me,' I begged. 'I'll make you tea,' I coaxed.

John arrived and I welcomed him with my usual tongue-in-cheek 'Sit down, relax, pull up a spider.' He studied my unwelcome visitor and, later turning to his reference books, was convinced that it was a small baboon spider – smaller than the other three in its immediate family, but big nonetheless, and venomous to man. His reference books told us that if bitten, the antivenin used for the black button spider's bite should be administered. It wasn't comforting to know that the black button spider is one of the most dangerous in southern Africa and that the nearest antivenin was only available 1,500 kilometres away. This simply reinforced my impression that spiders were aware of my aversion to them, and were out to get revenge.

John (with new alias Spiderman) lovingly mounted this charming specimen on a white sheet of paper, carefully labelled it, and offered it to me. 'You have to be kidding me,' I cringed in horror, taking a step backwards. It was a gift that I politely declined.

Years later, I watched one morning in fascination as a hunting wasp dragged a paralysed baboon spider, many times its size, across a sandy road. The wasp hauled the spider into a hole in the ground, where it would have laid an egg on it and the spider would have become a food source for the developing larva. I didn't like baboon spiders at the best of times, but this paralysed one had my sympathy.

It didn't change anything, however. I still loathe these creepy arachnids.

Soon after the baboon-spider incident, I drove with John to Hwange town to buy supplies, which was a round trip of more than two hours in his old Isuzu. I always slid into his passenger seat a little warily, my eyes darting around, checking for snakes and spiders. Something always happened whenever we were in that vehicle.

On this day, to my relief, it was just the radiator that sprang a leak. John huffed and puffed and muttered a few expletives as he pulled off the road, climbed out and lifted the bonnet. It turned out to be nothing that a little Trinepon putty couldn't fix. (It sets like cement and is used for fixing anything and everything, and there was always some in John's toolbox.)

While waiting for this precious commodity to harden, a herder walked past with his *mombes*. There was nothing unusual about that, except that one of his cattle was black-and-white striped. We looked, and looked again. That was definitely a zebra!

We spoke with the herder. The zebra had been with the cow herd for the previous five years but it was now causing some problems. 'It kicks the calves,' the herder told us. Surprisingly perhaps, this rural family had opted not to simply kill the zebra. They wanted it relocated.

We reported the matter to the Parks Authority but to our disappointment nothing was done to try to relocate the zebra to a suitable area within the park. I imagine it continued to kick the calves, but I never saw the herder again to ask.

On our way back home that day we stopped by the roadside to buy tomatoes – the ladies were always sitting there with their bright, sprawling pyramids of red – and as usual I wandered around picking up interesting seed pods from the ground, filling the floor of John's vehicle.

The seed pods of Africa's indigenous trees have always held a strange fascination for me. Perhaps most charming of all are the flat, woody pods of the pod mahogany tree. They split to reveal a striking bed of sizeable seeds, each one half-red half-black in colour, so very neatly housed, like little babies cradled together. The mountain mahogany is stunningly attractive when its pendulous, woody pods split into sections and curl backwards, giving the surprising appearance of a partially peeled banana. The circular pods of the mukwa, also known as the bloodwood tree, remind me of fried eggs. The fruit of the sausage tree is particularly impressive, dangling from great heights on rope-like stalks. They're said to reach sizes of up to a metre long and ten kilograms in weight.

It was sausage trees, a colleague confirmed, that were growing in my garden. There were *ten* of them. They were not particularly attractive at that stage, because their large leaves were stiff and brittle. When I had first moved into this rondavel it was surrounded by nothing but bare ground; the garden was subsequently planted by my own eager hands and a thatched fence erected. There wasn't a sausage tree, that I knew of, for scores of kilometres around. I was always sowing different types of seeds, though, enthusiastically gathered from here and there, to see what might just sprout. But I could never fathom what these particular plants could be. 'Sausage trees! Really?'

And then I remembered. In 2002, on our way back from Mana Pools – a World Heritage wilderness in the far north of Zimbabwe, where the Zambezi River separates us from Zambia – my girlfriends and I stopped by the roadside and I picked up one of these massive fruit, well over half a metre long. In typical girlie style we giggled at its phallic appearance and I decided that I just had to have one.

I brought it back to my garden, more for fun and display than for any other purpose; I'd never contemplated trying to grow a sausage tree. Some months later the termites, which were always around my thatched fence, built their home on it. The novelty had worn off by then and I thought no more about it. I do remember putting the hose on what was left of the enormous sausage, to wash away the termites. I don't remember scattering the seeds, though, so perhaps something else scattered them for me.

From just one sausage I had ten sprouting trees! For years and years I fondly watched them grow. Eventually, they towered tall and imposing in my lush garden, although the trunks and limbs were still very slim, and I longed to see the first pendulous sprays of deep-velvety-red flowers form.

I never got to see them flower or fruit however. I was evicted before that happened. It was the unforeseen, preposterous event of 2010. It was yet another battle that I had to face.

Evicted

After the successful scooping work that I completed in late 2009, and the onset of that year's wet season, the estate pans held plentiful rain water with promises that water would be pumped to them in the dry season. I decided that it was time to proactively help entice the tourists to return to Hwange to delight in the Presidential Elephants.

It wasn't that my wildlife conservation focus had changed; my outlook had merely broadened. I'd come to believe that the return of the tourists was crucial to the preservation of Zimbabwe's wildlife, including its flagship herd of elephants. Without the tourists, unethical sport-hunters and dodgy land claims would rule the wildlife's future. Despite everything that had already happened, I actively encouraged *all* lodges in the area to get involved.

South Africa's *Getaway* magazine approached me, and in November 2009 I was appointed their Elephant Ambassador in Africa. For eight months I wrote short pieces about the elephants, the environment and the surrounds for this popular magazine. It proved to be a superb way of sharing the uniqueness of the Presidential Elephants. In August 2010 I switched to writing online: a blog-page on *Getaway*'s website that reached even further afield.

Lodges surrounding the Hwange Safari Lodge, but never the Safari Lodge itself, began to promote the Presidential Elephants, taking advantage of my writings. Interest and bookings started to flow in.

I was accompanying some game-drives for these lodges on a complementary basis, as my time permitted, so that tourists with a special interest in elephants could enjoy more knowledgeable encounters. There was another good reason for me to occasionally climb on-board the game-drive vehicles: I wanted the safari guides to learn more about these elephants. They were not *just* elephants after all. There was so much known about them, many families were particularly habituated and all members were known as individuals. Yet uninformed guides stayed back more than 20 metres, which was the norm, and knew nothing more than general elephant facts. It seemed like the right time for this to change, although I was very aware that irresponsible actions could jeopardise both elephant and human lives. The guides and their guests would need rules to follow.

A few of the guides – especially those not threatened by a white, foreign female knowing more than they did about these elephants – were keen to learn, and having me on their vehicle now and then also meant that some of the really well-known elephants came to know and trust their vehicles more readily. It didn't take very long; the elephants, and eager guides, learned quickly. Guests who came specifically to visit the Presidential Elephants were thrilled with their close and informed encounters.

But the more people there were out on the estate, the more the failings in the estate management became glaringly obvious. Toilet paper and other rubbish blew around; people were allowed out of vehicles, scaring the game off for others; strange vehicles drove wherever they pleased, with people standing on open backs; and others were doing game walks much too close to these habituated elephants. It just seemed to go on and on. There were times when I felt embarrassed that I'd encouraged people to come and see sights like these. I wrote documents, flagged problem areas and made recommendations, but rules and regulations were never implemented and nothing was ever enforced. Repeated requests to speak with specialty estate and marketing personnel fell on deaf ears.

African Sun was responsible for managing this land. By the latter half of 2010 I was finally resigned to their indifference, but I continued regardless. I patrolled daily, always on the lookout for signs of poacher activity and snared animals, while picking up endless amounts of rubbish. I secured the expensive M99 immobilisation drug from Harare for use in animal de-snaring, and monitored the de-snared animals. A close eye was kept on water flow and the water levels of the pans. I monitored the Presidential Elephant families that I know so well, of course, recording interactions, new births, those in oestrus and musth, and anyone who was missing or injured. On request from various lodges, and as my time permitted, I sometimes jumped on game-drive vehicles.

It turned out to be an exciting and satisfying time and, most importantly, tourists were returning! There was also to be a one-hour television documentary filmed on my work with these elephants, with a proposed reaffirmation of the Presidential decree, which would be screened internationally. Zimbabwe, and Hwange, was finally going to receive some really positive press. It was particularly encouraging to see the increased interest from different lodges, from the media and from people who started to come back from all around the world.

Then, one day in September 2010, three African Sun head-office personnel arrived at Hwange Safari Lodge for a budget meeting. They'd asked to meet with me. Their marketing and estate personnel, those that I actually wanted to speak with, were notably absent. We talked for three hours, in the company of the general manager of the lodge, about the good, the bad and the ugly, and also about what I was doing for others and what I could, likewise, do for them. One of the men was supposedly documenting a way forward, based on the discussions in the room. What I was presented with the very next morning, however, after the head-office personnel had already departed, was nothing like what was discussed in that meeting.

The Hwange Safari Lodge GM handed me a sealed envelope. Inside was a two-page document titled 'Partnership Terms and Conditions – African Sun Zimbabwe (private) Limited and Ms Sharon Pincott'. Given that our meeting had ended at 6.30 p.m. and I was handed this document before 8 a.m. the next morning, I found it extremely difficult to believe that it hadn't been pre-prepared and that the three hours I'd spent with these men had been nothing but a waste of time. Had they simply been verifying their shopping list of demands?

To my bewilderment, the document stated that I was 'obliged to consent to abiding by the provisions herein within seven days' or I must 'vacate the Hwange Safari Lodge and Estate' within one month. They were threatening to throw me out if I didn't agree to their assorted demands. Those dragons had returned once more!

They were, in fact, insisting that I turn myself into some sort of unrewarded marketeer contracted exclusively to African Sun. If I didn't agree to this unpaid servitude, then the company would evict me from my tiny rondavel. (A different company initially organised for me to live in this absurdly small one-room rondavel with bare cement floor and rotten thatch roof, which had been my home for the past nine years. It had only ever been used as a storeroom prior to this, but I was prepared to live in it, so it had become my home.) They were also threatening to ban me from the land that I'd patrolled daily to the benefit of the Presidential Elephants, and had recently been responsible for resurrecting.

Despite having me on their doorstep for the past nine years, they had never shown any interest in working with me to conserve, promote or market the Presidential Elephants. They had never even requested my presence on their game-drive vehicles. Now they were insisting on exclusive, unpaid rights to my services!

The document was filled with astonishing demands, all of which made me feel like I was being forced into some sort of pitifully one-sided marriage. It insisted that I 'promote the Hwange Safari Lodge as the *preferred* destination for *all* Presidential Elephant tourists and enthusiasts', which I could never do, knowing that some tourists want a true 'safari camp' experience in preference to staying in a standard hotel. It also stipulated that I must '*only* serve the interests of the Hwange Safari Lodge and African Sun Limited'. It went on to say that I 'may not provide service, advertise or promote *any* of African Sun Limited's competitors'. These 'competitors' are in fact *every* other lodge in the area, and their guides, who I would now be forced to have nothing to do with. It also stated, rather ominously, that I was 'not allowed to influence lodge employees'.

It further declared that my previous unrestricted access to the internet/email – which was offered free of charge, and without restriction, to all of their day-time and overnight guests – would now be *reduced* to 'no more than two hour's access to email for any given three days in a week' at the GM's discretion. It also demanded that 'no emails should be directed at *any* of the corporate management'. 'Did they plan to censor the content of my emails too?' I wondered. And it introduced a brand new 30-day-notice clause on my rondavel, which could be served on me at *any* time.

Baffled, I glanced back at the title of this document. I hadn't been mistaken. It was unquestionably headed *Partnership*! I couldn't even begin to imagine how they might treat those with whom they had *no* interest in forming an alliance. This was no partnership, not even in the broadest sense of the word. This was an undeniable attempt to control and silence me. No reasonable individual, I thought to myself, would propose a document like this to an intelligent person. They were clearly used to dealing with people in a very different manner from what I was accustomed to. I considered their proposed contract to be nothing short of preposterous, and outlandishly arrogant. If they wanted a dancing bear, I reasoned, they'd do better to try the circus.

During the meeting with African Sun on the previous day there was never any mention of me working *exclusively* for their company. I was a wildlife conservationist after all, and a full-time volunteer! For the past decade I'd worked, unpaid and largely self-funded, for the good of Zimbabwe's flagship elephant herd, which certainly wasn't owned by them. Given their disinterest over the years, it wasn't surprising to me that they understood none of this.

I was very aware that they regularly referred to the Presidential Elephants as 'just one of the Big Five'. Now, all of a sudden, they were intending to *own* me. I was managing to help get tourists back into interested lodges in the area and African Sun didn't want just a piece; they wanted the entire pie.

The document and the demands were so outrageous that I couldn't even bring myself to consider discussing them. It was made very clear to those who chose to speak to some of the management team, with a view to better understanding the terms of their demands, that there was in fact no room for discussion.

I knew that I'd done, and was still doing, so much for the elephants (and for this company) on the land, as others knew well. In addition to the endless day-to-day tasks, it was only a year since I'd brought their pans, and therefore the wildlife, back to life and saved them more than US$18,000 in the process. There was no need for me to wait for their seven-day consent period to lapse. I immediately emailed that I would *not* be signing their pathetic document.

Carol and a friend arrived from Harare and shared in my bewilderment over this latest turn of events. Like Shaynie, Carol had seen me ride out the stormy waters of the past ten years. She had driven me around Harare several times over the years to meet with African Sun personnel, and knew how frustrated and disappointed I was with their ongoing apathy. We sat at Kanondo, recording data, and enjoying these incredible pachyderms; her travelling companion described the experience as 'other worldly'. On this day only one game-drive vehicle was out. We had the elephants to ourselves.

'You're the only one who looks out for these elephants,' Carol said staring sadly into the recently scooped pan, full of life-giving water and frolicking lumps of grey. 'They are what they are today because of your dedicated work over the past ten years. What will happen to them now if you're banned from monitoring them here?'

None of us spoke further. It was easier to gaze sorrowfully into the elephant-filled sunset, hoping for the best, but fearing the worst.

At the end of the seven-day consent period, while I was trying to make plans to move elsewhere, the Hwange Safari Lodge GM had one of his managers phone me to say that he wanted to see me. I assumed that this meeting would simply reinforce the 30-day-notice period, by now underway, and I walked unenthusiastically to his office and wasted no time in asking if he had an eviction notice for me.

'No,' he said, 'I want to have a talk.'

I sat down, surprised by this, looking at him but saying nothing, waiting for him to carry on.

'So, I've heard that you've changed your mind about signing our document,' he said.

'I haven't changed my mind,' I said, shaking my head.

'Well then, in accordance with our document, you have 30 days to vacate.'

I'd actually believed, for just a few seconds, that there might be an opportunity for dialogue.

There were a few more brief exchanges. I requested an eviction notice in writing. He declared that the document I already had made the eviction clear and nothing more in writing would be forthcoming. In the end I simply cut off his familiar ramblings, picked up my rondavel keys from the desk in front of me, stood up and said calmly, 'You know what, you're right. I really don't need anything more in writing.' And I walked out of that office.

He had simply wanted to talk *at* me, which I'd come to understand was pretty much the norm. He had arranged for one of his managers to be present in the office with us, so I should have realised immediately that there was little chance of him backing down since that would have meant losing face in front of a subordinate.

I was now tired, tired, tired of all of this continual … drivel. There was simply no other word for it, at least not one that was polite to use. When next I checked my emails there was a notice of eviction awaiting me, which I duly acknowledged.

* * * * *

As distressing as all of this was, it was the push that I needed to finally get out of the living conditions that I'd actually come very close to hating over the years. I was tired of living in a rural African compound with the constant loud noise of booming voices and blaring music and the filthy mess which I spent hours tidying and sanitising every month. There were light-fingered children, and items regularly disappeared from my 4x4 and garden. It was people's indifference that disappointed me most of all. It wasn't the same place that I'd moved into so many years before. You just had to look around to see that. It was only the elephants that held me there.

But where could I live now? Accommodation in the area was not easy to find and African Sun knew it. Feedback from other lodge owners and managers suggested that African Sun were actively doing their best to ensure that I had nowhere else to move to. One lodge offered me a temporary option on their leased grounds, but they withdrew it just days before I was due to move there when they found themselves on the receiving end of a perceived threat from Hwange Safari Lodge management. Others were apparently advised that I was a troublemaker at best, and that they should not allow me any accommodation or land access. It was curious, to the enquiring minds at least, that such a so-called troublemaker would be offered a partnership agreement in the first place! It appeared, after my refusal to sign their ultimatum document, that African Sun was merely attempting to save face at my expense. When people starting challenging their 'troublemaker' stance, they changed tack and allegedly told the Parks Authority management that I was irresponsible and had been leaving gates open on the estate. The only gates on the estate are those directly around the lodge itself, which meant that these arguments were quickly discredited. African Sun was struggling to offer plausible explanations.

I was prepared to take my chances on alternate accommodation rather than agree to sign a one-sided document that wasn't in the best interests of the Presidential Elephants, or tourism. I had no wish to be tied to African Sun, especially not with chains and padlocks, as was clearly their intention.

The big question was whether this group could stop my monitoring of the elephants, especially in places like the recently resurrected Kanondo where I'd always sighted the bulk of the snared animals. My mind overflowed with concerns for the elephants. Why would anyone *want* to put them at greater risk in this way? Game-drive vehicles are usually only out and about for a few hours of a morning and evening and their focus isn't on searching for distressed animals or monitoring wildlife. Nor are they out at the times when the snared animals are regularly seen. How many injured animals would go unseen now, left to slowly die, or be found later than they would otherwise be, their suffering prolonged? How many elephants would simply disappear without anyone even noticing? Clearly, these hoteliers didn't care.

Finally, it was very clear to me that I *needed* to move elsewhere. This was definitely not the sort of environment that I wanted to be trapped in. Due to the uncertainty surrounding my accommodation and land access, I resolved to pull out of the planned international documentary that was due to be filmed in just a few weeks' time. This was a real blow to Zimbabwe tourism. The filmmaker made it clear that there was no story without me in it, and people were encouraging me to stay on a little longer and participate. But how could I be expected to appear happy and positive on film under these unsettling circumstances? The documentary was cancelled, or at best, postponed. My time would instead be spent packing up and moving out.

I had nowhere to move to, no way to transport what I owned, with no clue about what I would do next. I gave many of my things away, I sold a few pieces of furniture for the pittance that I could get for them in the bush, and I burnt what was of no use to anyone else and couldn't be carried. I stored my 30-year-old 4x4 (nicknamed Nicki Mukuru), which wouldn't make it to Bulawayo, at my friend Henry's property in nearby Gwaai.

Standing outside in the flourishing garden that I'd planted and tended so lovingly, I watched the birds splash happily in my birdbaths. I gazed around at my beds of succulents and my colourful bougainvillea and the towering sausage trees. It was depressing to know that this would all, undoubtedly, revert back into eroded wasteland, as it was before I moved in. People here preferred to chop down shrubs and small trees (something that I witnessed all too regularly) and, as a result, their houses were surrounded by bare, eroded soil that they swept each day. It was just a whole lot more things broken.

'Masakhe,' I kept whispering, reassuring myself, remembering the little M family elephant wandering out there on the land. I wasn't ready to do it just yet, and I realised that it would take some time, but I knew that I would eventually rebuild. And when I did, it would be in a much more positive and supportive environment, away from the ludicrous demands of African Sun, or not in Zimbabwe at all.

The Bvumba's treasures

The Bvumba is the hidden jewel in Zimbabwe's crown. It's a beautiful place of rolling green hills in the highlands south-east of Harare; it's a place so unlike what you expect to find in Zimbabwe. In these picturesque 'mountains of the mist', close to the border with Mozambique, everything's lush and green. The enchanting forests are home to the elusive samango monkey and the colourful Livingstone's lourie. The Bvumba is also home to Tony's coffee shop.

'I am absolutely not going to pay US$10 for a single slice of cake,' I declared to Carol, who had taken me with her to the Bvumba to celebrate her birthday and to help me to relax after my eviction. That's a lot of money to spend on one slice of cake, especially when you've earned no salary for the past ten years. It turned out to be the best US$10 I've ever spent. Well, it would have been, had I actually been the one paying.

Carol loves Tony, loves Tony's coffee shop, loves the scrumptious selection of cakes always on offer, loves the list of hot drinks that's almost a metre long and especially loves the truly divine hot chocolates.

Tony waltzed over charismatically, and chatted with us. Who was this man who kept bringing a smile to my lips as he spoke? I kept consciously having to smother my grin, since I didn't want him to think me strange. In the end I avoided eye contact. Our quirky conversation was interrupted by customers requesting a photograph with him.

The slice of cheesecake that I'd hesitantly ordered appeared on light wings on the spotless white tablecloth in front of me. It must have stood 12 centimetres high, and was almost the same luxurious size in width. It was decorated with a fancy trellis of white chocolate and a huge, cascading dollop of clotted cream. I sat, staring at it. Then, still in somewhat of a trance, I picked up a spoon and ran it down one of the smooth creamy sides, all the way from the top to the very bottom. I slowly deposited the laden spoonful in my mouth, not aware that Tony was watching me. He'd stopped talking with Carol and had focused all of his attention on me.

'Hmmm, thank you, thank you,' he softly murmured. I hadn't said anything. I was in heaven. My eyes were, I think, momentarily closed as I slowly swallowed the exquisite taste sensation that I'd been leisurely rolling around on my tongue. I let out an audible sigh. 'Oh yes, thank you,' he whispered again, slowly nodding his head. Yet another smile split my face at the sound of Tony's voice. Where was I? Was I having some sort of sensual dream?

The cheesecake was wonderfully melt-in-the-mouth, made not just with cream cheese, but with cream and absurd lashings of white chocolate too. You put on three kilograms just looking at it.

I'd been to Tony's before, seven years previously in 2003, with my girlfriends Dinks and Shaynie. I just had to text Dinks, who now lives in South Africa, and email Shaynie, who wasn't in cellphone range. 'I can't believe that we didn't have a slice of cake!' I messaged urgently to both of them. Back then it had seemed outrageously expensive, times were tough, Zimbabwe dollars were short and we all declined to order cake. 'It's worth every single cent and more,' I prattled on.

The table of four behind us ordered just two slices of cake between them: one cheesecake and another that Tony simply described with rolling eyes as 'chocolate, chocolate, chocolate'. They didn't manage to finish their half portions, despite compliments flying and their cameras clicking. I, on the other hand, unashamedly demolished my entire piece, and was tempted to ask if I could take *their* leftovers home with me in a doggy bag.

Carol, who was savouring her own slice of something divine, wanted a taste, but I politely told her to bugger off. Mind you, after telling her to bugger off, I most charitably left just two mouthfuls on the edge of my plate so that she could discover for herself what all the fuss was about.

Eventually, we wandered (or was that waddled?) back to our

cottage, nestled high on a ridge, with soothing water views below and luxuriant forest all around. I plonked myself down on a comfy chair outside, wrapped a duvet around me to keep out the crisp air of the late afternoon, put my feet up and settled down with a glass of red wine to enjoy the changing colours of another mesmerising African sunset. Samango monkeys scampered unseen through the tree tops and a red-chested cuckoo sang his 'quid pro quo' song over and over and over again. For the first time in two years I found that I wanted to write seriously again, and it was here that I drafted the preface for this book. The Bvumba had quietened the rage within me.

Life here would have been just perfect, I thought, if only there were some elephants to enjoy ... and if only I'd brought home that doggy bag of cake.

Big, and Little, Fives

Africa's Big Five is somewhat of a misnomer to me. It includes elephant, the largest land mammal; lion, the largest carnivore; rhino, an endangered relic of times past; leopard, the personification of feline beauty; and buffalo, the largest bovid. 'Who', I've often wondered, 'would sensibly include the buffalo in such a list, before the likes of the beautifully sleek, lightning-fast cheetah?'

The Big Five is, in fact, a term coined by sport-hunters and has nothing to do with the magnificence of the animal. It actually refers to the most difficult African beasts to hunt on foot and the degree of danger involved. The tourists who come to the African bush merely to tick off the Big Five miss out on so much. We owe it to ourselves and to the wildlife to look further afield, at more than just these five large mammals.

I personally favour the Little Five, which opens tourists' eyes to the smaller wonders, and evokes a deeper appreciation of the world of wildlife. Instead of elephant, our focus is directed to the elephant shrew. Rather than lion, we seek out an ant lion. In the place of rhino, we look for rhinoceros beetles. Instead of buffalo, we admire the red-billed buffalo weavers. As an alternative to leopard, we keep a close eye out for a leopard tortoise. Suddenly, there's a whole new, miniature world to revel in.

Small and mouse-like, the elephant shrew has a long snout and large rounded ears. It's a solitary animal that feeds largely on insects, including the well-armoured dung beetle.

The adult ant lion is rather like a damselfly, but the term ant lion (also called a doodlebug given the trails, or doodles, that it leaves in the sand) refers to the rather ferocious larval form. These larvae live in pits in soft sand, awaiting prey such as ants to fall in, which are then grasped by tiny, but surprisingly strong, jaws.

The imposing horn of the male rhino beetle comes in handy when confronting its rivals during the mating season. Among the largest of beetles, they're shiny black and nocturnal.

The buffalo weaver is adorned with black plumage, white wing patches and a robust red bill. They're a social weaver, famed for their vast, untidy communal nests of twigs that festoon the branches of trees in the veld.

Just like Buddie, the leopard tortoise is a large, attractively marked tortoise that can, contrary to popular opinion, move surprisingly quickly.

Of course there are countless other smaller creatures that are equally enchanting, many of these most prominent in the wet season. There are the captivating fireflies, with a light-producing organ at the tip of their abdomen, usually found near water. There are the sweet foam-nest frogs with their soft chirping, that turn almost white in daylight, and the stunning emperor moths with large eye-spots on oversized wings. The longhorn beetles, with antennae longer than their strikingly coloured bodies, are comical – they squeak when they're handled. The curious, bright-red velvet mites, which appear with the rains, are the only arachnid that I'm really fond of. They look like tiny, velvet cushions. You don't have to particularly like them but the speedy Kalahari Ferraris, with their horribly long leg-spans, are deserving of a special mention too.

While not a great fan of singling out any Big, or Little, Five, since there are countless African wonders to enjoy, it's fun to create a little extra interest for people. If I were to choose Hwange's Big Five trees for example, I'd include the sausage tree (that once grew unexpectedly in my garden) with its huge hanging fruit. To that I'd add Zambezi teak, whose mass of stunning, mauve flowers on Kalahari sand brightens the summer months. Then there's the gnarled, bulbous baobab – the upside-down tree – one of the longest-lived trees in the world that looks strangely like its roots are in the air. To them I'd add the large false mopane also known in Zimbabwe as umtshibi, with its burnt-bark appearance and striking cherry-coloured coated seeds. Finally, I'd have to include the elephants' favourite, the *acacia erioloba*, whose velvety-grey seed pods are packed with protein and are one of their favourite treats.

John's very own Top Five intrigues me. It's a mixture of the big and little of the animal world. He loved Hwange and the African bush more than anything else. 'It was the love of my life,' he says frequently now with sincerity and longing. John belongs in the bush – belongs in Hwange – but when his Zimbabwean pension was buying nothing more than a small tin of his favourite mixed-fruit jam, he was forced to leave with only his memories for luggage. It was a deep-rooted loss that he's never gotten over.

Naturally enough, the buffalo is in John's Top Five. The one that gored him, but let him live, is etched forever in his memory. That creepy, hairy, thick-legged baboon spider made it in too, much to my horror but not to my surprise. Spiderman loves his spiders after all! Leopards make it onto his esteemed list too – that 'spectacular star of the bush' as he describes this magnificent, terribly persecuted cat. Alongside buffalo, baboon spider and leopard, John lists the ground hornbill – a turkey-sized bird blessed with one of the most evocative calls of the African bush, which I quickly grew to love too. It's a deep haunting song that I know John pines for every morning. The last in his Top Five is the African wild cat, whose facial expressions and vocal calls are much like that of a domestic cat. Similar to a tabby, but with orangey-red ears, one lived with John for ten years. It was friendly, playful and wary of strangers, its claws hooked firmly in his heart.

'Who then,' I find myself wondering, 'would comprise the Presidential Big Five – the most esteemed of the Hwange Estate's wild elephants?' With more than 450 extraordinary jumbos to choose from, all of whom are special in their own way and undoubtedly something more than one of the routine Big Five, it's a tough call. In the end I choose Lady, Whole, Misty, Inkosikazi and Skew Tusk.

Lady, now with same-sized tusks, leads the L family. She and her relations regularly gather around my 4x4 merely for company and often to sleep. I sing to her and she crosses her back legs and opens and closes her eyes so very slowly. It's a rare privilege to be part of the life of such a friendly, well-known family of wild elephants, led by an incredibly affectionate guiding star.

Whole, easily identified by the hole in the middle of her left ear, is particularly placid. She always chooses to stand very close to my 4x4, her trunk resting in an L-shape on the ground while rumbling intermittently, keeping a caring eye on her close-knit family. All of these endearing W ladies never fail to make everyone smile.

Misty is an exceptionally gentle giant who, like Lady and Whole, comes to me when I call to her. She is the proud mother of Masakhe. Now with a large tear in her right ear, Misty enjoys close contact and the comfort of my door, often standing within centimetres of my arm for over an hour. With no enticement other than my voice, she chooses to be there.

Inkosikazi is an enormous tuskless cow – one of five well-known big tuskless females – with easily identifiable notches in her right ear. Known since the 1970s, she's the undisputed 'queen' of the Presidential Elephants. Both she and Skew Tusk – whose peculiar right tusk twists under her trunk – are the two oldest of the original 22 elephants that formed the nucleus of what eventually became The Presidential Elephants of Zimbabwe. Both now estimated to be in their late 50s, they are legends who continue to ably lead their mild-mannered families through the changing seasons. Although neither of them seek out human company, they are certainly friendly and calm. If the sport-hunters and poachers keep their distance both will die of old age sometime within the next decade, which is a great achievement in these times.

These are five of the most renowned Presidential Elephants, but as with any Big or Little Five, there are scores of others equally deserving of special attention. It does indeed feel rather unfair to be singling these ones out. Nevertheless searching for the Presidential Big Five is a fun activity that elephant lovers can ardently pursue while on holiday in Hwange.

The demise of Grantham
– and Nicki Mukuru

After the eviction from my rondavel in late 2010, having not yet secured anywhere else to live in Hwange, I spent my time in the cities of Bulawayo and Harare. Nicki Mukuru, my faithful old 4x4, was sitting decrepit under a tarpaulin at Henry's humanitarian base in Gwaai. Her fuel consumption was a nightmare with the high price of petrol and she currently had no brakes at all, and a shattered back window after I reversed, tired and distracted, into the long low-hanging branch of a tree, which I swear hadn't been there the day before. If I was to return to Hwange, I would have to replace her.

During the weeks that I'm in Harare, on the hunt for a replacement 4x4, Carol and I encounter President Mugabe's cavalcade twice. They whizz past with such remarkably coordinated speed that I can't help but admire them. Everyone knows the tell-tale sounds, and drivers scurry nervously to get out of the way. Motorbikes zoom past first, with lights and sirens blazing, sending goosebumps down my spine. One patrolman stays for a short time at our intersection to ensure all traffic is halted. He then zooms off too and within seconds a string of police cars rocket past, their sirens also blaring. Then comes a knot of speeding black limousines, with blackened windows, driving two abreast. One presumably has the president inside. A troop of soldiers in sturdy helmets zips past next, sitting alertly on the open back of a truck, their machine guns at the ready. And finally trailing behind comes an ambulance, just in case, emergency lights flashing. There's no slowing down for this lot. Quite amazingly, they drive at this pace, and in this formation, all the way to where they're going. With busy intersections every few hundred metres, it's quite an achievement. I have no doubt that they'd drive right over you, if you were in their way.

'And all I want is a vehicle that isn't 31 years old,' I groan to Carol, wondering out loud if the president himself, sitting right there inside one of those posh black limos, remembers anything about the Presidential Elephants.

I'd recently drafted a short document for the president's attention – a reaffirmation of the Presidential decree that I hoped he might agree to sign – but I didn't even know what level within the presidential office my proposal had reached, and if anyone there really understood the benefits of Zimbabwe reaffirming its commitment to these special elephants.

For a few seconds I contemplate racing after him and asking him about it myself. But I'm quickly plunged back to reality, recalling the stern-looking troops with their machine guns.

The end of 2010 was fast approaching, and there were power cuts almost every day, sometimes for 15 long hours. With Christmas so close, this was even more frustrating than usual. To top off the year, reports of the sport-hunting of elephants *inside* Hwange National Park were now being openly acknowledged by some Parks Authority personnel. Photographic tourists and hunters, together in the same areas, simply don't mix. The hunters don't seem to mind but the tourists certainly do. This was crystal clear to me from first-hand observations of past chaos on the Hwange Estate. It was obvious that no lessons had been learned. It was depressing, to say the least, and once again I felt fed up with it all. There seemed to be no festivity in this holiday season, and I wondered if Hwange could even be called a national park while hunting was occurring within it. It just didn't feel like Christmas.

'Santa clearly doesn't know where Zimbabwe is,' I texted wearily to Henry in South Africa.

Quick as a flash, Henry responded, 'Santa doesn't go to Zimbabwe anymore. He's scared somebody will shoot his reindeers.'

After no success at the second-hand car dealerships, Carol's mechanic sent out word to the local 4x4 club that I was on the hunt for a reliable vehicle that wasn't too expensive. I eventually settled on a 1989 Land Cruiser wagon. A slightly younger, short wheelbase might have suited me better, but I consoled myself with the knowledge that at least I could sleep unrestricted in the back in the bush, if I ever found myself homeless again. The engine had recently been rebuilt and it promised better fuel consumption. I decided that I'd get the roof cut out to give it a Nicki Mukuru feel. Every used vehicle bought in Zimbabwe had to go through a change of ownership, a change of number plates and attracted a tax payment, and that process took weeks. In my case it turned out to be well over a month before all of the necessary paperwork was complete. Nicki Mukuru was named after a Bulawayo mechanic named Nick who made her roadworthy in 2001, and *mukuru*, which means 'elderly one', seemed appropriate. I was tempted to call this replacement vehicle *Mad* Mukuru. Many Zimbabwean processes and logic were incredibly frustrating and no longer amusing to me.

* * * * *

January 2011 arrived and I was still in Harare, planning my return to Hwange while trying to finalise the purchase of my 4x4. I was missing the elephants, but seriously wondering (once again) how much longer I would stay in Zimbabwe, when news of what was going on in Australia reached me.

Tragedy struck on Monday the 10th of January with virtually no warning. A wall of water 8 metres tall hit with deadly ferocity, smashing into homes in the small, farming community of Grantham in Queensland, where I'd spent the first 17 years of my life. This was no ordinary flood; it came with deadly speed and fury. The press was calling it an inland tsunami. Many people had been swept to their deaths.

'Why haven't they evacuated Mum and Dad?' I blurted into the phone to my sister Debbie the next day. 'Just because their house is still standing doesn't necessarily mean they're okay.'

Debbie was only 30 kilometres away from Grantham, in the city of Toowoomba, which had also been hit by severe flash flooding, although she may as well have been in Africa with me. She couldn't get anywhere. All roads leading into Grantham were closed. Phone lines were down. My eldest sister Gene lived closer, in the small township of Placid Hills right next door to Grantham. She could see helicopters making roof-top rescues, hampered by pouring rain, but the magnitude of the tragedy wasn't yet understood by anybody. 'There are obviously others in more urgent need,' Gene texted me on my mobile.

Far away, and not comprehending the gravity of the situation, this made little sense to me. The torrent of water that levelled the town had hit on Monday afternoon. A second flood hit on Tuesday and by Wednesday afternoon we still didn't know for certain that our parents were okay – a reflection of the turmoil in the town – although Gene could see that water levels had receded. Everyone was thought to have been evacuated by then, but our parents still weren't out. Grantham was cordoned off; no one other than emergency personnel was allowed in. In darkness, at 10.30 p.m. on that Wednesday night, emergency-services personnel boated into my parents' built-on-stilts elevated home and finally confirmed that they were all right, although they were without electricity, drinking water and plumbing. They would be evacuated the next morning in daylight.

It was an emotional and nerve-wracking time for my family, although compared to others, my parents had been relatively lucky. With two metres of raging water underneath their home at the height of the flooding – water that was filled with swirling trees, vehicles, houses, concrete water tanks and masses of other debris – their house could easily have been knocked from its stumps, with them inside. Only now did they learn the extent of the fate of their friends and neighbours, of the many houses that were destroyed and others that floated away, of the myriad vehicles thrown through the water like matchsticks, of people stranded inside houses and vehicles screaming for help, of precious lives lost.

A convoy of army trucks rolled into Grantham to join the police and emergency-services teams already there. The town was designated a crime scene while the gruesome search for bodies got underway.

It was nine days after this catastrophe struck that the 350 or so residents were finally allowed into what was left of their homes, but it would be many more long weeks before my parents could return to live in theirs. The once-picturesque town resembled a war zone. It had been smashed to smithereens. There'd been destructive flooding over much of Queensland, but Grantham was at its epicentre, the 'ground zero' of these devastating floods.

Australia Day – celebrated on the 26th of January every year; a day to rejoice in being Australian; a day to enjoy an Aussie barbeque and a few beers with friends and family – was commemorated with a memorial service in Grantham, rather than the usual festivities.

A week later I flew out from Zimbabwe and landed in Australia. Grantham was still in lockdown, although it was finally reopened to the general public a few days later, one month after the tragedy struck. Weeks of cleaning and clearing by hundreds of soldiers and emergency-services personnel using heavy equipment had already been underway, yet I couldn't believe what I was seeing. The scale of the devastation was shocking. The brutal ferocity of Mother Nature was evident everywhere. It looked like a bomb had gone off.

I recalled the words I'd written in a story a few years earlier:

I come originally from Grantham, a tiny country town in the Lockyer Valley in sunny south-east Queensland – the largest of Australia's eastern states. I lived there as a child on my parents' vegetable farm in a wooden house perched on wooden stilts, prudently designed to catch the breeze. The sprawling fields outside sometimes lay freshly ploughed, although they more frequently boasted a cover of bright green leaves as far as my young eyes could see.

The Lockyer Valley was now being referred to as the valley of lost souls. My parents' house was still there, perched high on the wooden stilts that had saved their lives. The sprawling fields outside, and their large lush garden, had been turned into a sea of deep, stinking mud, littered with piles of debris. A kilometre away there used to be a functional general store, a fuel station and a pub. Now there were piles of rubble, deserted buildings and eerie spaces where homes had been. It felt like a ghost town, especially at night when dark shells of houses haunted the road through the forlorn little town. Official words, scrawled in pink paint on building after building, emphasised the tragic tale: 'Unsafe. No entry.' The rubbish and dirt, the broken fences and ruined houses made it feel like the bowels of a Third World country. The great Aussie spirit was legendary, but I wasn't sure how people would recover from this. Politicians remarked on the community's 'toughness' and I was thankful to have grown up in this neighbourhood; I'd needed all of this toughness, and more, to endure all that I had during my years in Zimbabwe.

My parents were still taking stock of their losses, underneath and around their home, and their luck. They'd received a phone call just ten minutes before the flood water reached Grantham, warning them of water coming their way. Not realising the fury of what was heading for them, my mother jumped into her car to take it to higher ground; another vehicle was organised to bring her back home. But by the time she'd parked her car and was making her way back, the initial stages of the raging torrent had arrived. All of a sudden she found herself waist-deep in wild water but, luckily, managed to get safely back to the house. Had it been just a few minutes later, this outcome would likely have been tragically different.

I suffered my own personal loss. My entire pre-Zimbabwe life was stored underneath my parents' house. My father had built a storage shed for me, with a raised cement floor. Crates laid on that floor meant that everything was stored above the highest flood level that my father had ever known. But this was a flood like no other. All of my possessions had sat drenched in filthy water and stinking, thick sludge for nine days while no one was allowed into the town. They were sodden, ruined and broken. Gene and Debbie had collected what was salvageable and painstakingly washed and scrubbed the little that could be saved. I could only shake my head at some of what survived. Scores of beautifully framed photographs and original prints and paintings were destroyed, literally hundreds of books and photo enlargements and thousands of photos spanning nearly 50 years of my life were all ruined and yet a half ream of useless bond paper was untouched and gleaming white. I couldn't even work out why I'd packed it at all. My old four-bedroom household of designer bedding, plush towels and cushions had been packed in boxes. What survived of these unscathed was a pair of bright-red towels that I had never liked and never used. Perfectly intact too, with not a hint of water or mud anywhere, was an envelope full of insurance photos of my household contents for annual insurance that I'd paid religiously for the last 25 years; I'd cancelled it just 3 years previously, when donor funds had dried up and fuel money to enable daily Hwange Estate patrols seemed a more important place to direct my ever-dwindling savings. I picked up a gleaming black mug and stared at it with a sinking heart. In white writing around its outer surface it read: 'Life's a bitch. Then you die.'

I had packed up my Brisbane home ten years earlier. I worked alone and it had taken me many weeks. I'd then hired a truck and transported my contents north for private storage. Over the years, as circumstances changed, I moved the scores of boxes and packages to a rental storage shed, and later hundreds of kilometres south to my parents' home in Grantham, and finally to the specially built shed underneath their house. I'd nurtured my belongings, sorted them, checked on them regularly whenever I was home, but for what? It all now seemed like such a waste of time and effort and money. So too all those years of taking, sorting and enlarging so many thousands of photographs. I hadn't actually lived in Grantham for 30 years, and hadn't used any of my household items for the 10 years that I'd been in Zimbabwe. I wasn't known by many as a flood victim, and I knew that there were lots of people worse off than me, but I still felt a very real sense of personal loss. During my years in Zimbabwe, material possessions had become far less important to me, but it was a sinking feeling to no longer have these possessions to fall back on. And there were all those irreplaceable photographs and books and letters and diaries, now lost forever.

Hundreds of army personnel provided vital assistance to Grantham's massive clean-up effort. To many in Africa, the word army evokes fear.

It's a four-letter word, the puppet of dictators and the armed forces of corruption. But in Australia, military personnel are ethical, highly trained defenders and peacekeepers; they are the elite who expertly assist when needed with search and rescue and disaster relief efforts at home and overseas.

The debris around my parents' house had been so extensive that the tall back staircase was completely blocked, and there was the stench of deep, thick silt everywhere. As an indication of the degree of devastation and debris, the mud and the misery, caused by the wild torrent of water that had arrived so unexpectedly, a contingent of army personnel 30-strong were assigned one day to help my parents with their clean up. They assisted them greatly in their efforts to return their home and their lives to some degree of normality.

I thought again about the little elephant named Masakhe. In Grantham too, people were attempting to rebuild what had been broken.

Karen, my hippo-friend, emailed and suggested that perhaps it was a sign that Zimbabwe was where I was meant to be, where I was meant to stay. But I wasn't nearly so sure, despite struggling with First World life. I couldn't get the microwave to start; I couldn't work the iron with its strange steamer attachment; I didn't know which button to press to answer the phone, before realising that I didn't have to press any button at all. I felt unsure of so much, and strangely insecure. My New Zealand friends, Eileen, Andrea and Bobby, had also been in regular email contact since the Grantham disaster struck. Their support and concern was heart-warming.

There were, however, more dramas in store for my family. My 77-year-old mother, attempting to get her beloved garden back in some semblance of order, dropped a lump of concrete onto her foot and smashed three toes. My niece, Rebecca, had only just moved to North Queensland and quickly found herself directly in the path of Cyclone Yasi, which devastated the township of Tully. My nephew, Matthew, in flooded outback Queensland, was stricken by a waterborne disease associated with cattle and found himself recovering in hospital. I started to wonder if someone had put a spell on me ...

And then came news of more shocking devastation. Christchurch in New Zealand, home to Eileen's family, was hit by a deadly earthquake on the 22nd of February, just five weeks after the Grantham catastrophe. Close to 200 were feared dead and much of the city was in ruins. I'd lived in Auckland, in New Zealand's North Island, for five years and travelled often to Christchurch, in the South Island, on business. Emotions were already too close to the surface, and I found myself once again struggling with a dreadfully heavy heart. I needed to go and walk on a beach.

When I arrived in Maroochydore on the Sunshine Coast – three hours away from Grantham by bus – it was raining. It didn't matter, though. I didn't need sunshine; I just needed a bit of peace.

Crabs scurried sideways at my approach, taking shelter under outcrops of smooth, black rock sculptured by wind and water. Rare streaks of sunlight turned darting seagulls to silver, and for a few minutes an incredibly bright and beautiful double rainbow enveloped the rolling ocean. I stooped to pick up tiny seashells and gazed at the colourful kite surfers, their kites dazzling even under cloudy skies. Rainbow lorikeets – stunningly bright, multi-coloured parrots – and eye-catching pink and grey galahs squawked in the trees that adorned the sand dunes. There were plovers and ibises, and even a female kookaburra raising her fluffy young, while some folk fished quietly from the beach. Standing still in waist-deep water, letting the foamy waves wash over me, I breathed deeply and felt months of stress roll off my shoulders. I was startled when the head of a cormorant popped up in front of me. For a second I had thought it was a sea snake. I found it extraordinary that he was choosing to fish in these choppy seas, his sleek, agile form ducking and diving under the waves. The name Maroochydore comes from the Aboriginal word *Murukutchida*, meaning 'home of the black swan'. I didn't see any black swans, but my encounter with the graceful black cormorant wouldn't be forgotten in a hurry. I savoured every bite of my seafood meal that night and fell asleep to the calming rumble of the ocean and its cool breezes.

It was a little further north, just off Australia's eastern coastline, on Fraser Island – the world's largest sand island and now a World Heritage wilderness – that I learnt to love the sea. It was here too that my father (later bestowed with the motto 'Fish fear him' by his mates) taught me how to catch fish when I was still just a youngster in primary school. My three sisters and I fished for tailor so big that two of us girls were forced to team up with one line. While one of us struggled to reel the fighting fish into shore, small fingers sliced by the weight of the line, the other stood with arms stretched high, helping to keep the line pointing skyward. I became expert at catching incredibly long, slimy, beach worms, feeling the arch of their bodies and knowing exactly when to pinch my fingers tightly together, drawing the worm that was sometimes taller than me, higher and higher, out of its home in the sand. If still on the hunt for more bait, we'd do the twist in the wet sand, using our bare toes to feel for the smooth, closed shell of a eugarie. Dart and bream enjoyed the eugaries best of all and I would gaze sadly at the many whiting, caught with the worms, swimming around in hastily constructed shallow pools of seawater, staying fresh while unknowingly awaiting our sizzling frying pan. Cyclonic weather sometimes turned the ocean wild, and waves crashed furiously against rock and sand. It was after such fierce displays of nature that I'd walk the beach alone, skipping over clumps of seaweed washed up on the sand, on the lookout for shells – especially the beautifully spiralled triton shell, the giant of them all. Prior to Fraser Island being declared a national park, and such activities being declared taboo, we took them home with us and displayed them proudly. The destructive forces of nature were never far away, even back then, with droughts, floods, frosts and hail storms often on the horizon. I thought it beautiful when my father once brought a potato plant home from our farm, dripping with long, glistening icicles, unaware of the great hardships that nature frequently caused. Mother Nature could be so very beautiful, and so very cruel. Lately, she'd claimed far too many lives.

As I walked the beach, remembering when Andy and Lol had holidayed with me on Fraser Island the year before Andy died and recalling too how they'd loved to walk together on the beach, I thought about a poem I'd once read. It said that what mattered most of all was the dash between our date of birth and our date of death. I reflected on this, as I hadn't really done in years. It was so very true. It really doesn't matter what we own. All that matters is that we're truly content with how we spend our dash.

It was difficult to recollect my life in landlocked Zimbabwe; a life a million miles from this peaceful beach; a life that I wasn't feeling particularly keen to return to. Was Zimbabwe where I wanted to continue to spend my dash? I just didn't know. There were sure to be more dragons there, albeit of a different kind. In my troubled Africa, it wasn't Mother Nature that I had to be constantly watchful of; it wasn't she who persistently tried to thwart my efforts.

I sat on the soft, white sand and flicked through the pages of a local newspaper. Just for fun I read my horoscope. Taurus (the stubborn one) for the 5th of March 2011: 'Work-wise, your crap-tolerance threshold is lowering every day and it's hitting bottom by April ...' I could only raise my eyebrows and groan. Was I returning to Zimbabwe to just more of the same?

One week after I left Grantham and flew back to Zimbabwe, the devastated town was once again in lockdown. This time it was for a festive occasion. Its residents were treated to a right royal visit; it was a welcome distraction, and a real comfort to many. Soon to be married in spectacular style, Prince William arrived in this tiny town – a town which most of the world's inhabitants had never heard of just ten weeks before – to lift the spirits of a broken people.

Another new beginning

I flew from Australia into Harare, wondering what the rest of 2011 might have in store for me. I needed to collect my recently purchased Land Cruiser from Carol's home and drive it to Bulawayo, and then on to Hwange. I was going back to start again. There were still more battles than needed to be fought.

All hadn't gone according to plan in my absence, though. The cruiser's roof had been cut out nicely, but the roof-cover was a disaster. It was like Victoria Falls inside my vehicle. Rain water pooled on the cover with just the slightest shower, and the cover itself was made of old tarp that leaked like a sieve and would only get worse in time. It had also been cut far too small, so that rain poured in from both its front and back. My crap-tolerance threshold was indeed about to hit rock bottom.

I used tube after tube of silicone and eventually resorted to getting one end of the cover extended, and better secured, using wide Velcro, which was a mission to find in Zimbabwe. It took days of patching, gluing and drying time before I was satisfied that I finally had a partially waterproof cover that would have to do for now, but which would eventually need to be completely remade and refitted. Carol had very kindly contributed elephant-theme seat covers, and better tyres, and eventually I was on my way in my new beast – Mad Mukuru.

Following my eviction from the rondavel, I'd stored what was left of my Zimbabwe household at Shaynie's flat in Bulawayo. I collected what I could from there and headed north towards Hwange. I was bound for Miombo Lodge (which has since been refurbished and renamed Miombo Safari Camp).

Miombo had recently been bought by a partnership and, fortunately for me, they understood the value of wildlife conservation. After hearing of my plight I'd been kindly offered a cottage to live in. It was a very generous offer of ongoing support that I'll always be grateful for. At the time, Miombo had no permission to do game-drives among the Presidential Elephants and so they didn't directly benefit from the herd at all, making this offer of assistance especially charitable.

When I first arrived in Zimbabwe in 2001 I lived on the grounds of Miombo Lodge for a short time. There had been two different owners since then and a lot had happened and changed. I felt a sense of déjà vu moving back. It was like my African life had gone full circle. I'd started off at Miombo a decade ago and now I was going back, to begin again.

Miombo is the Swahili word for *brachystegia*, a type of tree of which there are numerous species. Miombo woodland is an important vegetation type in Zimbabwe, dominated by trees belonging to the bauhinia (*caesalpiniaceae*) family, one of which is *brachystegia*, which includes the stunning msasa (*brachystegia spiciformis*) and mfuti (*brachystegia boehmii*) trees. Other prominent miombo woodland trees include munondo and cassia. I was thrilled to see that the feature tree in my new front yard was a towering munondo, renowned for its colourful spring-time new-leaf foliage, which, similar to the msasa, ranges from browns to pinks to purples (but not to the eye-catching bright reds of the msasa), shifting eventually to the usual shades of green. Msasa, bauhinia, combretum, kudu-berry and teak trees are also prominent around my cottage. It would be a pleasure to live in a place where the native trees and shrubs aren't routinely chopped down. Snakes, though, are said to particularly favour miombo woodland (also known as msasa–munondo woodland), which isn't great news for me.

My cottage is located in a secluded spot, surrounded by all of these trees, a few hundred metres from the lodge, and has its own entrance off the tar road that leads to nearby Dete. Nobody (at least nobody human!) had lived in it for many years. Mike, one of the partners assigned to oversee the refurbishment of the guest lodges, was not yet based there to be able to warn me about all of the many things that needed to be fixed up.

A couple of attractive pot plants had been thoughtfully placed at my front door. When I opened it, though, the pungent smell of urine hit me right between the eyes. I involuntarily wrinkled my nose and walked in. It was a proper little house and nothing like the tiny one-room rondavel I'd lived in for so many years. For that, I was extremely grateful. A sizeable white bucket, almost half full with fat drops of water, sat ominously on the floor beneath the geyser. (Having lived in New Zealand for five years I need to clarify the word 'geyser', since my friends there will immediately wonder how I can possibly live with a geyser in my house. Be assured that it's not a hole in the ground, shooting steaming hot water high into the air at unpredictable times, which is the only kind of 'geyser' that my friends Down Under know. In Zimbabwe it's merely a hot water system.)

There was another worrying stream around the base of the toilet and yet another around the nearby sink. I peered into the shower. I couldn't imagine ever feeling clean after bathing in there. 'Easily fixed,' I thought to myself, quickly averting my eyes and looking around for something a little more encouraging. I glanced up, and cringed. Patches of sunlight were visible through the rotting thatched roof. I breathed deeply, and told myself that all would be fine, eventually.

That evening an army of giant praying mantises fluttered in through a broken window. I actually like praying mantises, but this was a winged invasion. I decided to shower and take refuge under a mosquito net. The hot water was cold, and while dancing a bit of a jig under the chilly flow I managed to stand on a scorpion. It was a tiny little fellow and as I grasped the soft ball of my foot, cursing, I remembered Hippo Haven and the lesson learnt there that it's the small ones that are usually the most lethal.

Wanting the day to be over I flopped into bed – a real bed, in a bedroom that was mine, for the first time in ten years – and tucked the mosquito net in, especially tightly, all around me. My throbbing foot, combined with the continuous drip, drip, drip from the peculiar geyser and 44-gallon drum setup perched high under the A-frame thatch not far from my bed, and a horde of overly active rodents that emerged immediately after the light was off, meant that sleep did not come easily.

'The dripping geyser is going to drive me nuts,' I lamented to Craig, who runs a small grocery store in Dete, when he thoughtfully arrived the next morning to help me settle in. I was rubbing my bloodshot eyes and feeling very sleep deprived.

Craig brought along Amos, his odd-job man, to try and devise a plan. Amos is a lean 27-year-old father of one son. He has no teeth at the front of his mouth. If you ask him what happened to his teeth, he'll tell you that an insect started from the front of his mouth and is still going.

It was quite a mission, Amos discovered, to empty both the geyser and associated water drum, disconnect them and lower them to ground level. There were hoses and pipes everywhere. We had all presumed it was the geyser that was leaking, but eventually discovered that the geyser was in fact fine. It was the 44-gallon drum, which sat on top of the geyser, that had been leaking steadily onto the wooden support rails and down onto the floor.

So the main chore now was to repair the drum. I couldn't quite fathom why it had been positioned there in the first place, but I was assured that municipal water could be unreliable here and a small private reservoir was especially useful.

'Arrh, this drum, Madam,' announced Amos, 'it is dead.'

'There are no other drums Amos. You need to try to fix it,' I insisted.

'But you can't fix dead, Madam.'

How could I argue with that?

Amos used a soldering stick, straight out of the red-hot coals of the fire he made in my front yard, to apply silver solder to hole after hole after tiny hole.

'Arrh, but there are too many leaks, Madam,' Amos kept muttering quietly.

'Last one Amos,' Craig eventually declared, trying hard to be encouraging.

But of course, inevitably, another new leak sprang to light. Amos rubbed his forehead. The day was fading and by now I had a throbbing headache too.

'Let's get this all back up in the roof,' said Craig, now also visibly tired.

I looked up into the roof. Nothing had changed; I could still see the sky. At least I hadn't seen what Craig had a few hours earlier – a giant mother rat with baby, scampering through one of the holes. 'That rat was as big as a cat,' Craig smirked.

'I can't afford to rethatch the entire roof right now, but I do at least have to get these holes patched,' I groaned.

'You think?' Craig whispered, looking skyward and shaking his head.

The ache in mine was becoming decidedly worse.

Amos was sent to Hwange town to purchase a pane of glass to mend the broken window in my living room. It was just a standard-sized window but he measured and remeasured it methodically. He appeared the next day at my cottage carrying a compact parcel. Craig walked in front of him, once again shaking his head.

'You don't want to know what's in that package,' Craig muttered to me.

I glanced down at the parcel, which was wrapped sturdily with both cardboard and tape. If that was the window glass it certainly wasn't the right size.

'That's the glass?' I asked tentatively.

Amos, in all his wisdom, decided that it would be easier to carry if he had it cut in half …

'Amos! How does this glass fit my window nicely now?' I challenged.

'You just put putty, Madam,' said Amos, 'across the middle. And also use some Trinepon glue.'

Wearily I closed my eyes, and bit down hard on my tongue. Massaging my forehead, I was at least now certain that I was back in the Hwange bush. I thought of John. Trinepon had been his universal fix-it product too.

'I'm telling you that with the next rains, this place is going to be Victoria Falls,' exclaimed Craig, once again gazing high into my thatched roof, 'and it won't be the geyser that you'll be stressed with.'

'Oh great,' I sighed, 'Victoria Falls inside my Land Cruiser *and* inside my cottage.'

Thankfully the rusty water drum was now (sort of) fixed and, much to my relief, there were no more serious drips from there. It was time to move on to the roof problem. I needed a young man named Thabani, a thatcher who lives in Dete.

'Please Amos, will you tell Thabani to come and talk to me tomorrow.'

'Yes, Madam. That is no problem, Madam.'

I cringed. All of this 'Madam' stuff made me feel 200 years old. When I asked Amos to call me Sharon, he insisted that it was much more polite to call me Madam. So that's what Amos continued to call me, and I continued to cringe.

The next morning dawned fine, following another splendid evening for rats and mice. My rodent intruders came in many different shapes and sizes, and they'd all apparently laid claim to a slice of my cottage. The all-night party they'd just enjoyed meant that I was once again sleep-deprived and feeling somewhat on edge.

If you've ever observed the acrobatic talents of a mouse, you'll know that they're really quite impressive. I watched one little fellow scale one of my candle sticks and balance precariously, tail wagging like a dog, on the very tip of it. He fell off and climbed up again, only to repeat the exercise four times, seemingly just for fun. Then he found himself on top of a brick and for a good three minutes didn't seem to be able to make his way down to the floor. He was starting to irritate me. I was about to climb out from under my mosquito net to help him, but as I moved he jumped and landed with a loud plop on the dressing table. By now, resigned to my fate, I found myself laughing out loud at his antics. If I didn't laugh at all of this carry-on, I thought, I might just cry. I couldn't help but imagine myself succumbing to bubonic plague.

Thabani arrived, bright eyed and hopeful of some work.

'This roof, it needs to come off. It is rotten,' Thabani exclaimed.

'No, Thabani, for now you just need to patch it for me please.'

It would be another two months before the local ladies began their annual ritual of cutting thatching grass in the veld, and there was little left in the area from last season and certainly not enough to thatch my entire roof. Right now, still unsure of what lay ahead, I wasn't prepared to invest in a complete rethatching job anyway.

'This roof it is very little all over,' insisted Thabani.

'Yes, Thabani, I know. It's rotten and it's thin. But for now we have to just patch it,' I persisted, 'even though there are giant rats in it too.'

'Rats?' Thabani queried, his eyes shifting skyward.

And then, precisely on cue, the performance commenced. There we all were, Thabani, Craig, Amos and me, standing in the living area and staring up into the A-frame roof, watching a huge rat cavorting on the wooden beams.

'Look at the long tail on that thing,' declared Amos.

'I think it likes to be looking at the stars up there through those holes,' offered Thabani.

By now I could only roll my eyes and groan.

'Please Thabani, get a thatch cap on this roof by tomorrow afternoon,' I pleaded.

Craig's early morning arrivals were by now becoming routine. I used to welcome friends into previous abodes with the words 'Sit back, relax, pull up a spider', or perhaps 'Sit back, relax, pull up a snake'. Now I welcomed them with 'Sit back, relax, pull up a rat'.

Craig came armed with tools and paint and putty and cement … and rat poison. By chance, he found a chair to sit on, rather than a rat.

I'd bought clay birdbaths from the roadside in nearby Gwaai, and Craig helped me install them somewhat creatively in my front yard. Why was I not surprised when neither of them managed to hold water for longer than an hour?

I'd been forced to leave behind ten years of thriving plants at my old rondavel, but was grateful now to have a couple of new owl- and elephant-shaped clay planters. I wandered over to the lodge, bucket in hand, to collect a little soil. Everything around my cottage appeared to be pure sand. As I used my hands to scoop up some dirt, a wriggling baby cobra slithered right beside my fingers.

It was 2 p.m. on my sixth day back in Hwange and I desperately needed some red wine. Forget the glass, by now I was ready to drink straight from the bottle.

How God could have created the world in seven days I really don't understand. It took me, along with two, and sometimes three, other helpers, a good ten days to make my cottage barely habitable!

Thabani did a great job patching and trimming the thatched roof. It actually looked half decent. How badly it still leaked remained to be seen.

The place still smelled of urine, rat urine as it turned out, so I went with Craig to Hwange town to buy disinfectant and more rat poison. On the way back we stopped to buy watermelons by the roadside. In Australia there are 'honesty boxes' beside crates of produce on the roadside in which to place your payment. In Zimbabwe you're mobbed by half a dozen or more dishevelled folk, frenzied by lack of business, all desperate to sell their single melon, their baobab fruit, their enamel dishes full of tomatoes or perhaps 'African sweets' – a tiny brown wild fruit with a cream-coloured seed inside, that doesn't taste too bad.

Along with the watermelon, I decided that I'd like a wooden chair to sit on under the leafy trees in my front yard. I agonised over where the curio sellers were getting their wood, but decided that I'd buy a chair, so long as it wasn't more than US$20.

'Absolutely,' Craig agreed. 'Those chairs aren't worth any more than US$20. Don't pay a cent more than that.'

We placed our posteriors on many a chair by the roadside, but none were particularly comfortable. There was this one chair, however, that stood well over a metre tall, attractively made with a classy elephant carved into its back, and with a seat of a decent size and shape.

'How much is this one?' I queried, trying not to appear too keen.

'US$50. It is a fair price,' announced the owner of the chair nonchalantly.

Both Craig and I told him that he was crazy and that we weren't interested in tourist prices.

Soon the price was US$35.

'It's still too much,' I declared, walking away, my negotiating skills well tuned.

All of a sudden Craig piped up, taking the side of the owner, before I had a chance to negotiate further.

'It really is a nice chair. There's a lot of work in that chair.'

'It's too much,' I insisted, glaring at Craig out of the corner of my eyes, giving him a look that could kill.

'No, really, it's worth it,' urged Craig.

'I can't afford to pay US$35 for a roadside chair,' I reiterated, shaking my head.

'This chair won't be here if you come back. You'd better take it now,' Craig insisted loudly.

I stood and stared at him defiantly, smothering a grin. What the hell was going on here? All of a sudden I was negotiating, in front of the owner, with the person who'd just assured me that anything more than US$20 was too much to pay for a chair; the same person who was supposed to be supporting *my* negotiation!

'You realise that now we're negotiating with each other, instead of with him,' I pronounced, in earshot of the owner who by now wore a huge smile on his face.

Craig had taken the extra US$15 out of his wallet.

'Craig! What are you doing?' I blurted out, walking further away.

'That one really likes this chair,' I heard the owner whisper to Craig.

We drove away, me still shaking my head. And I shake it every time I look at the chair, standing proudly in my living room, since a chair that pricey can't be left exposed to the outside elements.

The leaking toilet and bathroom sink still had to be repaired. I could no longer even look at what was being done. Nothing ever went smoothly in the African bush, and just glancing at the previous plumbing work gave me the creeps.

'Why are the palms of your hands so black Amos?' I queried.

'Arrh, Madam, it is the putt,' declared Amos.

Confused for a second, I looked down and spotted a packet of putty. It was indeed black. I decided that I needed to go outside and leave Craig and Amos to it.

A troop of vervet monkeys was visiting, visibly nervous at the sight of a human. I talked to them and bobbed my head up and down in affable gestures.

'Arrh, friendly human,' they seemed to say. They appeared rather delighted at this apparently unusual concept and were soon sitting calmly in the trees.

'Are you winning, Amos?' I heard Craig ask.

'No, it's okay,' Amos responded.

'What exactly did that mean?' I wondered. 'Yes, it's okay, or no, it's not okay?' I wandered further away.

Craig walked into the front yard with a huge bobbejaan spanner in hand. Like me, he'd obviously had enough of the bathroom leaks for a while. While he was standing under a shady tree, cigarette in hand, there was a loud plop followed by considerably louder cursing. I moseyed on over to see what had happened.

'That was close,' Craig grumbled. 'If that bloody monkey had shat *on* me you would have known about it,' he smiled.

I looked up, grinning from ear to ear and secretly praising the monkey. It must surely have been karma for Craig not sticking to our agreed chair-negotiation tactics!

There'd been countless bizarre happenings over the past week, not the least of which was a couple of monster ants that climbed the hose pipe to the geyser tank and lodged themselves inside a nozzle, completely blocking the flow of water. By the tenth day, though, everything was starting to look up. Craig and Amos were exhausted (I don't know what I would have done without them), and I was thrilled. I now had mended windows and locks, a tiled shower tray and hand-built towel rack, a welded gate and security bars, a painted front door and shower, a cemented doorstep, functional power outlets, working geyser, toilet and sink, not to mention birdbaths that didn't leak. I also had a tidy thatched roof and polished cement floor, and an almost-empty box of crack-filler. Most things in my cottage still looked rather tired, but hey, I did now have brand new basin taps and a toilet handle. The setting outside was tidy and peaceful. The rat population was gradually declining. I decided to decorate with brightly coloured African fabrics and lots of cushions to give my new abode a vibrant, trendy look inside.

Life was good, I eventually decided, looking down at my rubber flip-flops that had deep rodent teeth marks all around their outer edges. I'd opted to keep them as a souvenir. They would be an interesting talking point of life in my new home.

There was still one thing that troubled me, though. I'd joined the ranks of those who swept their yards. This, in time, I'd have to rectify. In the meantime, I'd take pleasure in the private leafy outlook and the splendid birdlife.

It was full moon, and I sat on my doorstep with the stunning ball of light visible through the tree tops and savoured a glass of red wine. Happily, after all of these harrowing, and often hilarious, days, I no longer felt compelled to drink straight from the bottle.

Days of décor and averted disaster

I sat bolt upright in bed, massaged my temples, and muttered out loud to nobody, 'Oh, man. Are you kidding me?'

Now I had *bats*. Two of these pint-sized creatures flew overhead, round and round and round. It was 2 a.m. The windows of my cottage were all closed but there is a small ventilation hole, uncovered, high on the wall in the bathroom. They must have winged their way in through that. 'Great,' I mumbled to myself resignedly. 'Now it's sit back, relax, pull up a *bat*.'

Perhaps I wouldn't succumb to bubonic plague after all. Perhaps I'd die of rabies instead. I buried my head beneath my pile of soft pillows and tried to coax myself back to sleep. But I could still hear them skilfully navigating the dark night, cutting the air with remarkable speed.

The next day was a décor day.

The mornings had become quite chilly and I slipped my feet into somewhat grotesque, overly fluffy slippers and padded to the kitchen to make myself a slice of toast. I very nearly stepped on a dead rat, which was sprawled on the floor in front of my fridge, covered in ants. 'At least there's no squirming, fat, maggots this time,' I murmured to myself, lifting it up by its tail. I was getting quite used to this by now, although the thought of eating anything had suddenly lost its appeal.

Tiny dust particles caught my eye, illuminated by the morning sunlight streaming in through my open front door. The shimmering specks of dust were sitting directly underneath *that* wooden chair. 'Now you *are* kidding me,' I muttered, eventually getting down on hands and knees to have a closer look.

Craig arrived with drill in hand, and without any pleasantries I pointed to the controversial chair and blurted out with a laugh, 'I paid premium price for added extras. This chair's bursting with wood borers!'

'Oh,' said Craig. And then, after a long pause and peering down onto the dust-covered floor, he added, 'Hungry, aren't they?'

After dustings of *Doom: Blue Death* (what could possibly survive a name like that?), and streams of spray from a can of *Baygon*, the borers were soon on their way to wood-borer heaven.

I thought of Nicki Mukuru. She was on her way to heaven too – 4x4 heaven. She was still sitting at Henry's humanitarian base in Gwaai. When I'd gone to retrieve the last of my tools, she looked so very old and tired and dented and broken and rusted that I was pleased that I didn't have to try to start her. After ten years of reliability and loyalty, she was no longer mine. A Bulawayo mechanic had actually paid me money for her, much to everyone's surprise, which would help a little with fuel expenses. I'd left her sadly, recalling how much the elephants loved her, clutching the faded leather steering wheel cover that John had hand-tooled for me a decade earlier, which I just couldn't leave behind. I was eager to see how the elephants would react to my replacement vehicle, but first there was decorating to be done.

Amos drilled holes into my cottage's thick, concrete walls for curtains and hangings while Craig sketched a colourful elephant motif at the top of my newly painted front door. I still held onto something else that was a decade old. When I first lived at Miombo in 2001 their resident safari guide at the time expertly crafted two pieces of wood for me, each with an elephant figure at its end. One spelt out the name *Thandeka*, the other *Mandlovu*. Together they mean 'much-loved mother-elephant'. They were now given pride of place, hung on the outside bricks beside my front door.

Inside, I sealed more cracks with crack-filler, applied paint to walls and covered the cement floor with fabric and grass mats. I burnt incense and scented candles to encourage a more pleasing aroma while arranging and rearranging my furnishings and knick-knacks.

The cottage was finally starting to take on a welcoming air. Perhaps as a result of having lost so much in Australia, I felt a need to try to transform it into a real bush home.

For the past decade I'd made do without luxuries like an electric kettle, a microwave, a fan and a heater. There was nowhere to put them in my previous tiny abode. Next time I was in Bulawayo, I decided, I would indulge in a few items that would help make my life a little less taxing. I'd lived so frugally for so long and, given my new appreciation for how things can be taken away from you in a flash, I decided that I should try to make my day-to-day life a little easier.

Amos looked around at my elephant candle holders, the elephant chair, the elephant ornaments of varying shapes, sizes and colours, and the elephant wall hangings. 'There are elephants everywhere in this house,' he blurted. 'What about a giraffe?' I picked up a bright yellow cushion with a giraffe painted on its cover, and threw it at him.

After noticing, with a shudder, a short, plump snake slithering across my sandy yard, I decided that I could also do with some snake screens; I just wanted something to position across my front and back doors when they're open, so that snakes couldn't slip inside quite so easily. Amos nailed together a wooden frame and some old, rusty, metal gauze, and splashed on a bit of paint.

'Your snake blockers are done now, Madam,' announced Amos, clearly starting to believe that this white woman had some rather peculiar desires. 'What about one for your *bedroom* doorway now, Madam?' he offered, with a grin.

Ignoring his cheeky sarcasm, while suppressing my own grin, I decided that it would be really very pleasant to have a braai pit outside, beneath the leafy trees. It was comforting to know that I finally had some space of my own and somewhere to sit with friends. So the men set to work yet again and dug a shallow, round pit, and then plastered it with cement. It was a smashing success.

'You can fill this thing with water when you don't want a campfire and you'll have a better waterhole than some landowners manage to maintain,' declared Craig. 'It'll make an excellent birdbath.'

'The elephants can come here and drink too, Madam,' Amos contributed.

'We should have a braai once this work is done,' I proposed. 'We could invite the elephants.'

'We'll have to make some really strong chairs then,' said Craig with just a hint of a grin. And then he added, 'We'll serve them Amarula'.

'Yes,' Amos chuckled long and hard, 'yes, that's what we could do. They would like that I think.'

We might have been working our butts off but for the first time in years in Hwange I was having a regular laugh.

The cemented braai pit did in fact end up as a giant birdbath, which the colourful kingfishers enjoyed immediately. A few days later, shovel in hand and drenched in sweat, barely able to breath, I gained a renewed respect for my male helpers after I laboriously dug another braai pit myself, close by in the rock-hard ground.

I set to work creating a bit of a garden too, trying for some semblance of greenery. It would, I knew, be a welcome sight when the surrounding bush became stark and grey and bare during the winter months.

My home improvements were finally complete and I longed to get out with the elephants. I was sitting outside at a wooden dining suite that Craig's girlfriend, Bev, had kindly bequeathed to me (neither of us minding that the harsh weather, and the termites, would forever alter its appearance), wondering how I would tackle my next hurdle: land access. All of a sudden there was a thunderous explosion, followed by ominous crackling, coming from my cottage. I raced inside, sending a chair flying in the process. The electricity distribution box, mounted on a wall in my bedroom, was on fire. Long, orange flames licked skyward, towards my thatched roof. 'Fuuuuck!'

The only other words that came to mind were 'Help!' and 'Fire!' which I bellowed repeatedly, while hastily moving my bed from beneath the flames, and then attempting to extinguish them with a blanket. It didn't seem to be doing much good, though, and I dashed outside and bellowed again. Sprinting back inside I did the only thing I could think of. I put my hand through the flames and flicked off the switches on the distribution box, before whacking the flames some more and then racing outside yet again, the palm of my hand now blackened, to bellow yet again. I sounded like a wounded buffalo. By now some of the lodge staff were running towards me. Thankfully, though, the flames were out.

My blackened bedroom wall told the tale. The flames had reached to less than 30 centimetres below the thatched roof. Had my roof gone up, my whole cottage would have, with all that I owned inside it, and then perhaps the surrounding bush, and maybe even the lodge too.

Was somebody trying to tell me something? For months now it had felt as if someone had put a spell on me, although I was quietly confident that my juju would turn out to be more powerful than theirs.

My cottage was chock-full of thick smoke that didn't seem to want to budge. I borrowed a fan from the lodge, and opened all of the windows and both doors wide. Somebody was already attempting to fix the electricity box.

That night, power finally restored, I was feeling decidedly uneasy. Although everyone seemed to have an opinion, nobody had actually properly determined the cause of the fire. Would this scenario repeat itself, while I slept, my head resting on pillows right below the blackened box? Smoke still choked the air, and although I did shut the doors at nightfall, I kept the windows open, planning to close them before I drifted off to sleep. There are security bars on my windows and so, although preferring to keep the windows closed at night, I didn't feel too vulnerable. I lay on my bed with the lights off, remembering that I still had to close the windows, and then promptly fell asleep.

At 2 a.m. I awoke with a start. Somebody was creeping around inside my cottage. I could hear movement, and strange sounds that I couldn't identify. I plucked up the courage to climb out of bed and headed for my bedroom doorway. It was pitch dark and I used my hands to feel my way. I stood at the doorway and listened. I heard nothing. So I inched a little further towards the kitchen area.

All of a sudden I collided with something unknown; my leg brushed against some sort of horrible, strange, furry being. 'Fuuuuck!' I got such a fright and jumped so high that I must nearly have hit the roof.

What the hell was in my house now? I dived for a light switch. And there was Chloe, the lodge cat, who had to my knowledge never even visited my cottage since I'd moved in, looking up at me and meowing innocently. 'Chloe,' I sighed, bending down to pick her up, and now laughing wildly. 'You crazy cat, you scared the living daylights out of me. Don't you ever do that again.' Chloe merely meowed for a second time, and looked rather pleased with herself.

I recounted these happenings to the lodge staff in the light of day and everyone thought it hysterical. But my windows are well over a metre and a half off the ground. How did Chloe, now 13 or more years old, manage to jump that high?

'Chloe can even open a door. She jumps up and uses her paw on the handle to open it,' I was told proudly. 'So she can leap into your windows easily.'

That wasn't particularly comforting. I've never left my windows open at night again.

I bought yet another tin of white paint and a new brush, and revamped the blackened wall. 'What could possibly happen next?' I wondered.

Back with the elephants

It was with trepidation, rather than excitement, that I ventured out onto the estate, after six months away. I desperately wanted to find out how the elephants were faring but at the same time I felt waves of anxiety, deep in the pit of my stomach. 'What dragons were awaiting me now?' I wondered.

As I drove around, I steered clear of Hwange Safari Lodge. Unless the lessees of that lodge changed, I decided, I wouldn't go back there, even for a drink. If nothing else, I had learnt the truth in the adage: 'People might forget what you did and people might forget what you said, but they will never forget how you made them feel'. African Sun, if only momentarily, had made me feel like my past decade of work with the Presidential Elephants had been a waste of time. They trivialised it all. I knew this was only because they were so far removed from it that they simply didn't know any better, but given their callous treatment of me I saw no point in wasting any more time on them. If I had been permanently forced out of the area by their actions, so much already in the planning stage would have been lost for these elephants.

It had been a generous wet season and there were pleasing amounts of surface water lying around. Now that the rains were over, the water in these non-pumped depressions wouldn't last for long. The cement trough that feeds Mpofu pan was bone dry. No water had been piped into this pan, which I'd painstakingly organised to be scooped in 2009, for months; probably not since I'd been forced out. Nothing had changed. Mtaka, another of the key pans scooped in 2009, was in an even worse state. The safari operators who drove their guests around this land were making no effort to keep water flowing. Once, it had flowed year-round.

It was exasperating that operators charged up to US$50 per person per game-drive, and yet they weren't putting any of it back into this land or the wildlife. Even if they had no genuine concern for the wildlife's welfare, you would think they'd be motivated to sustain these scenic waterholes regardless, if only for the greater enjoyment of their guests who do appreciate a choice of waterholes for wildlife viewing and evening sundowners. But this, apparently, wasn't a good enough reason to do anything either. I had only just returned and already I was trying to fathom the unfathomable.

I still had to verify whether African Sun could in fact stop me from going to the State Land area of Kanondo, as they'd stated was part of my eviction, so for now I opted to stay away, as frustrating as this was to my daily monitoring. It would be difficult, I knew, to find all 17 of the Presidential families in the other land areas that I'd frequented over the past decade. I'd have to find new areas to traverse in order to give myself more daily opportunities. For now, though, I concentrated my field time around Fosters, Mtaka and Mpofu pans.

There were a few favourite elephant families that I was particularly keen to find. In my absence, Lol, from Lady's family, was due to give birth to her very first calf and I longed to know how she was coping. Echo from the Es should also have given birth to her first calf, around the same time as her mother Eileen was due to deliver another little one. Assuming all had gone well, Whole too should have a new baby beside her. There were lots of births to record but these ones held extra-special interest for me. Of course I was also eager to catch up with Misty, Masakhe and all of the Ms, to see how everyone in that family was getting along. The moment I stumbled upon my first family I experienced a sense of overwhelming joy and the stresses of the past six months instantly lifted from my shoulders.

It was the C family that I came upon straight away. Matriarch Cathy is one of the majestic tuskless cows who is always charming and amicable. Don't believe those who say that tuskless elephants are aggressive. It's something you hear frequently in Zimbabwe, repeated blindly by all and sundry, but I believe it to be a myth of the uninformed.

They may sometimes be aggressive, but only because the ignorant fear, and consequently frighten, them.

Courtney, with a large square notch in her right ear, is the friendliest of the Cs, apart from her son Court that is. He's a loveable and somewhat bold boy who simply doesn't want to leave his relatives. He's taller than both Cathy and Courtney, which puts him in his very late teens. (A male of 17 stands taller than every female in a population.) Most males leave their family, either of their own accord or when they are pushed out by the older females, at around 14 years of age. Yet here's Court, approaching 20, and still with his mum. His trunk is frequently dotted with war wounds, although I've never noticed anyone in his family bullying him. These battle scars are more likely from brief encounters with independent males, which must have convinced him to stay at home with his mum and siblings for as long as possible. He's a big softy at heart after all.

Courtney recognised my voice at once and came trotting over to investigate, looking a little confused. She stood right beside my door. 'What are you doing in *that* vehicle?' she seemed to be asking me. While I stood up through my open roof, the Cs investigated my bonnet and back window, apparently satisfied that it was indeed me back with them once more.

* * * * *

It was in the midst of a warm, sunny day that I found the entire W clan milling around Mtaka pan. I held back, searching through my binoculars for Whole. She wasn't there. I didn't carry out a proper census but *everybody* seemed to be there. Everybody except Whole. I drove forward and called to Whosit, to Willa, to Wilma, to Why, to Wonderful, and to so many of my special girlfriends. They came bouncing up to my 4x4, huge heads waggling, not caring at all that I was in a different vehicle.

'Where on earth have you *been*?' I'm sure I heard them say, as they poked their trunks inside my windows, pressed their tusks on my bonnet, nudged my bull bar, grabbed my side mirror, peered in through my open roof, squealed and rumbled, and generally had a happy time welcoming me back.

I was thrilled to be among them once again. But where was Whole? Had she died in childbirth? Was she sick? Had she been snared? I looked at Whosit's son (Whole's grandson), Wish, and felt another rush of intense concern. Wish didn't look at all well. He was thin and much smaller than he should have been. He tried constantly to suckle from his mum but she wasn't moving her front leg forward to allow him to do so. He was only a year old and wasn't getting sufficient milk. Whosit, it seemed, hadn't turned out to be a very capable first-time mother.

I spent three hours with the Ws that day, hoping that Whole would appear. When she didn't I moseyed on home, concerned but quietly hopeful that she'd simply wandered into thick bush before I arrived, and that I'd catch up with her soon.

A few days later I raced home to email my new-found friend Tru (who lives in France), barely able to contain my excitement. 'Whole's got an adorable baby girl, and *you* get to name her,' I gushed.

Whole had brought her lovable little daughter to the door of my 4x4. It was as if I'd never been away. She was as serene as always, and we slipped back into our usual relaxed routine, enjoying a quiet chat through my open window. Her little one was already adventurous, trunk up and kissing the side of my 4x4 and then wrapping her tiny proboscis around the lower rod of my bull bar.

I emailed photographs to Tru, who then thought long and hard about what this special little girl would be called. She emailed back these words:

> This little girl is very welcome and wanted by me. She is the future. She WILL BE our new hope for the Presidential herd and a beginning of a better time with less poaching, threats etc – and freedom for you to do your job.

Tru named her Will-be.

* * * * *

When some of the As materialised around Mpofu pan one morning I immediately searched for Adwina. It was almost a year since Esther removed the ghastly wire snare from her leg and there was a slim chance that she hadn't recovered. There she was, still not walking 100 per cent well and the wound very obvious even now, but she was fine and she had a new baby girl beside her.

Esther is of Dutch origin, just as Tru is. She was temporarily in the Netherlands with her family, preparing to defend her PhD thesis in the presence of an examining committee. In Dutch, Esther told me, a small elephant is an *olifantje*. The last syllable of this word – Antje – is also the name of a little Dutch girl in traditional clothing, made famous through her presence in television commercials in the 50s and 60s. And so this little elephant, who would never have made her appearance into this world had it not been for Esther's skill in darting and the careful treatment of her mother, was lovingly christened Antje.

* * * * *

There'd been two successful snare removals from elephant bulls in my absence. No one had thought to take identification photos, though, and while I'd seen photographs of the sedated bulls lying on the ground I had been unable to identify them from these particular angles.

I found myself one afternoon at Mpofu pan with tuskless Debbie, who now leads the D family after the sad and mysterious disappearance of matriarch Disc. I noticed Dempsey, a teenaged bull, with a snare wound. The wire was thankfully off, but he was still limping quite badly. The wound on his back left leg matched some of the photographs I'd seen. 'I'm sorry Dempsey boy,' I whispered.

The snaring situation wasn't as grave as it once was, but it was still there and probably always would be, despite the efforts of the anti-poaching teams. At least now we knew who one of the recent victims was, and I could monitor his progress. Until this point in time

Dempsey had been just another de-snared elephant, whose progress was unknown.

* * * * *

With the Ds that day was the F family, lead by matriarch Faith. She'd broken her very long and unusually straight right tusk and for a moment I didn't recognise her. My mind drifted to her namesake, who'd only recently got back in touch via my website after eight long years. It was such a surprise to hear from her. When I lived on the grounds of Hwange Safari Lodge she was my neighbour for a while. She and her husband Tafadzwa moved to Zanzibar in Tanzania. They'd had two daughters – one of them named Thandeka. Faith told me that she still cherished the photograph of Faith with offspring Freddie and Fantastic that I gave to her a million years ago.

'I wish I had followed to the elephants' watering hole every day,' she wrote. And then, 'I miss your laugh. It used to drive me crazy.' She'd obviously been gone for a very long time indeed, I reflected. I couldn't remember the last time I really laughed while living there. It didn't matter, though. What mattered is that these elephants, and this special family in particular, are still firmly wedged in her heart all these years later.

* * * * *

There were good-news stories to be had, but no matter how much time I spent in the field I couldn't find Lady and her family. I wondered constantly if they were alright, and if any more lethal snares had been inflicted on any of them. They'd certainly endured their fair share. They clearly move in areas where snaring is, or at least has been, rife. I worried about them all, and kept wondering if Lol's first baby was okay.

Eventually I caught up with the Ms and the Es, who are closely related and often move together. It was lovely to see Misty again. She came when I called to her, but hung back a metre or so, not ready to offer me her complete trust again just yet. Masakhe was beside her, happy and healthy, now two-and-a-half years old. He had become a little legend and I talked to him, telling him what a special little elephant he is. His cheeky response was to kick sand at me with his hefty front foot.

There was both happy and sad news to record for the E family. Eileen had a fine-looking little baby boy beside her. He was later named Elvis, a true King of the savannah. But something terrible had happened to Echo's baby. Echo no longer had any breasts, and there was definitely no baby. Did she miscarry? Was her baby stillborn? Did it die after birth? We would never know now, but Echo's baby was gone forever.

Lady and her family were still nowhere to be found.

Reaffirmation of the Presidential decree

I n days past it was Florence Nightingale who tended wounded soldiers. Now it was Florence Nhekairo who tended wounded elephant conservationists. Along the same lines as 'the lady with the lamp', I privately dubbed this woman 'the lady with the beacon'. She became a ray of hope for me.

It hadn't been easy, but finally, after numerous phone calls and faxes, I secured a meeting in Harare with Florence, Permanent Secretary to the Minister of the Environment and Natural Resources. I needed to gauge the current degree of high-level support for me, and for the Presidential Elephants.

'Do those elephants still exist?' Florence asked me doubtingly. It was immediately clear that I had a lot of work to do. Florence and I talked for an hour and a half, about the elephants, about previous land claims that had so negatively affected them, about the snaring problems, about the pan scooping that I'd finally managed to complete, about the safari operators who continued to pump insufficient water, and about my eviction. Most importantly, we talked about the possibility of the president reaffirming the Presidential decree. This was my new mission: to persuade President Robert Mugabe, via this Ministry, to reaffirm his commitment, and that of his office, to the ongoing protection of these elephants.

I left Florence that day with a draft of what the president might consider signing. I longed to see something in certificate form this time, so that there was finally something tangible for the general public to read. Florence promised to lend a hand, with support from Minister Francis Nhema.

We exchanged various text messages after that, and I continued to fax and email relevant information. Nothing is ever as simple as it sounds, though, especially in the Hwange bush, and I battled with broken or non-existent printers, photocopiers and fax machines, and frequent phone-network outages, all of which drove me to distraction. I wasn't getting the feedback I was hoping for, and was considering making the tedious eight-hour journey back to Harare for another face-to-face meeting.

Then, quite unexpectedly one day, I received a text message from Florence that read, in part, 'Am pleased to advise that His Excellency the president signed the reaffirmation decree.' I read this sentence three times before I leapt to my feet, let out a boisterous whoop of joy, did a little dance, grabbed a bottle of champagne from my fridge that I'd bought in Bulawayo just a few weeks before on the off-chance that this might eventually happen, popped the cork, and drank straight from the bottle! I grabbed my mobile phone and texted those who I knew would share in my excitement. 'He signed it. He actually signed it!' I gushed. I was beside myself; I was giddy with a surreal feeling of astonishment, gratitude and deep satisfaction. And champagne, I know now, tastes so much better when you drink it straight from the bottle! It was an incredibly thrilling moment, and one of my most satisfying in the past decade. It was one of those rare moments that I knew I must commit to memory, to recall later, when those dreaded dragons returned once more.

A few weeks passed before I managed to see the signed document. Alas, somewhere along the line during the editing process, the words 'Hwange Estate' in the first paragraph had been altered to read 'Hwange National Park', which actually wasn't quite as it should be. But the sentiment was still there, loud and clear, and it wasn't the time to be picky. It wasn't professionally typeset as I'd been planning, but it was signed by the president and further sanctioned with his seal. It could be scanned and enlarged for framing.

This is what the president put his signature to:

In 1990 – under my patronage and as a symbol of my personal commitment, and that of all Zimbabweans, to conservation and wildlife management – the elephants that roam the Hwange National Park in Western Zimbabwe were declared protected. They subsequently became known as The Presidential Elephants of Zimbabwe.

It is my great pleasure, twenty-one years on, to reaffirm this Presidential decree and Zimbabwe's commitment to the ongoing protection of this extraordinary clan of wild elephants.

The Presidential Elephants have earned their place as one of Africa's great wonders. Visitors to our country marvel at close encounters with these wild free-roaming giants. Tourists compare these exceptional creatures to the magnificent mountain gorillas of our East African neighbours.

Like governments everywhere, we are faced with the challenges of balancing the conflicting needs of man and the environment. Zimbabwe has a sound wildlife management infrastructure, combined with the capacity to recognise the need to protect this exceptional resource.

I pay tribute to the invaluable contributions made by all of us to the ongoing preservation of this flagship herd. It is our responsibility to ensure that these elephants continue to roam freely within the wild beauty of the Hwange Estate.

I reaffirm my patronage and that of my office, to this unique elephant herd.

It was signed Comrade Robert Gabriel Mugabe, The President of the Republic of Zimbabwe, 19th of May 2011.

Hal-le-lu-jah! Hallelujah, hallelujah! Not exactly as I'd envisaged, but it was all done and dusted. I still couldn't quite believe it. Sceptics asked me if it really meant anything and I was quick to assure them that it did. In the 2003–2005 period, when I fought for the return of Hwange Estate land, which a government official had claimed as his own to hunt on, I did so for these elephants. It was primarily because they were the *Presidential* Elephants that this battle was eventually won. If ever land claims raised their ugly head yet again, there was now an updated reminder that this was *Presidential Elephant* land, that sport-hunting was taboo here, and that the president had recommitted to protect this unique wildlife resource. Shockingly, there were already rumours of coal-mining rights being issued within the key home range of the Presidential Elephants, around the Dete Vlei, very close to the photographic Sikumi Tree Lodge. If ever this turns out to be true, the reaffirmation will surely help with this battle too. Without my regular monitoring of the Presidential Elephant families, no one knows if they are all roaming safely or not. Some clearly still didn't want my eyes and ears, and certainly not my outspoken voice, in the field and I constantly wondered what they had to hide. Only if land owners and lessees got away with disrupting, and indeed preventing, the monitoring of this flagship herd of elephants in their land areas would President Mugabe's decree reaffirmation end up meaning nothing, since they are not well-versed, or dedicated, enough to properly monitor these elephants themselves.

My next mission was now clear: I needed to ensure that this reaffirmation got the publicity that it deserved. The South African film crew were back on the scene and the international documentary on my life, work and relationship with the Presidential Elephants was the ideal platform to accomplish this.

Whatever had died inside me was slowly reawakening, morphing into a renewed sense of purpose, into something better than before. Things were finally moving in the right direction, and they were advancing with leaps and bounds.

A *week in another*
wilderness

Scaredy-Cat. That's my friend Shaynie's radio call sign at Wilderness Safaris, who have four luxury photographic safari camps on two wildlife-packed private concessions in the far eastern corner of Hwange National Park. She moved from Bulawayo and started working there, in the back offices, in late January 2010.

For someone who loves the bush Shaynie is, for the most part, terrified of her country's wildlife, especially under the inky cover of darkness. She resorts to earplugs. 'Sometimes it's best not to know how close the lions are,' she shivers, conjuring up within the dark recesses of her mind those apparently awful and worrisome deep-throated bellows. I can't understand it. It's one of my favourite sounds in the world, the closer the better. Inside her staff accommodation on the plains, she has an escape route all planned.

'With two steps I can be on top of a cupboard, and from there I can climb into my roof,' she declares.

I picture her, knees around her ears, huddled in a corner of her roof, scarcely breathing, waiting anxiously for the lions to leave.

'How do you figure that lions will get *inside* your lodgings in the first place?' I ask her incredulously.

She doesn't have a plausible answer and I giggle at her and shake my head in bewilderment.

'I'm going to outlive *you*,' Shaynie retorts, with just a hint of a smile.

I imagine she's not just referring to a potential lion calamity. She's been privy to most of my Zimbabwean dilemmas, after all. She probably would outlive me, I conceded, but I still had visions of her in old age, all hunched over and crinkly and mute, as a result of having spent too much time squashed, and deathly silent, in the roof of her staff quarters.

As a guest of Shaynie and of Wilderness Safaris, I spent a magical week in this unforgettable part of Hwange. I hadn't been back for long, but a lot had already happened and I figured I deserved a short break. I packed a duffle bag and took a leisurely drive, through the national park, from Miombo to Ngweshla picnic site, where I would leave my 4x4. I take this route too infrequently and I revelled in the change of scenery.

I made my way down a sandy, corrugated, road lined with umtshibi (large false mopane) trees, and eventually passed the base of the Parks Authority's Wildlife Capture and Relocation unit that shares this same name, Umtshibi, where Andy once worked. Driving by here always brings back a flood of poignant memories. I stopped a little further on at Makwa pan, one of my favourite spots inside Hwange National Park, where 10 years before I had scattered the ashes of Chloe, my beloved canine friend who shared 18 years of my pre-Zimbabwe life. I parked by the water's edge and nibbled on cheese and crackers. I was already in holiday mode.

With time on my hands, I moseyed on towards Kennedy Vlei, and pulled up with a smile to gaze at a group of 11 grand elephant bulls doing their thing. They were boys just being boys. They strode magnificently through golden grass to water, under clear blue skies.

I arrived at Ngweshla earlier than my scheduled pickup time and took the opportunity to drive around the loop roads, where surface water still sat from the summer rains. I came upon 6 ground hornbills in the company of 20 noble elands and more than 30 zebras. One of the zebra stallions caught my eye immediately. He had a trellised 'saddle' over his back, extending down to both sides of his body. Rather than being neatly striped, he was adorned with an intricate lattice of squares, rectangles and circles. This boy was beautifully unique. It was just the beginning of the beauty that was to come.

I was collected by Lewis, a Wilderness Safaris guide, who was cheerful and lively, and full of smiles and the joys of spring. It was a one-hour game drive to Little Makololo Camp, where a delightful surprise awaited me. Wilderness is always quick to snap up some of the best guides, and there to greet me was Sibs, an ex-Hwange Estate head guide. I hadn't seen him for eight years.

It didn't take long for our excited conversation to turn to the one thing that we knew we could laugh about together. And that was John Foster. We'd been privy to all of the same stories: of John naked on his rooftop, of spitting cobras on his bed, of spiders and of buffaloes.

When John left Hwange, Sibs bought his deep freeze. I sipped my welcome drink and listened to yet another amusing Foster tale.

'I'm sad to be selling this deep freeze,' John had lamented to Sibs. 'I've been studying this spider for a long time,' he said pointing to a hazardous-looking creature living in its back. 'You can buy this freezer, so long as you take care of my spider.'

Sibs assured him that, of course, he would look after the spider, which John claimed, with a grin, was a 'double-claw fridge dweller'. Then Sibs made his way home, pleased with his deep freeze purchase, and promptly dispatched the unwanted arachnid.

At Little Makalolo I felt instantly at home.

Little Mak is a delightfully intimate camp with just six luxury tents. The lounge and dining areas are open to the elements and have been built under smart canvas, separated by a towering umtshibi tree. I liked that there was no thatch. I'd had my fill by now of rodents scurrying around in grass roofs. I wolfed down a scrumptious lunch in the company of Sibs (food-wise I'd become easy to please, but there was no disputing that this was delicious), while Meyer's parrots chirped in the tree tops, and impalas, baboons and a bull elephant enjoyed the camp waterhole.

Trainee manager, Shayne (not to be confused with Shaynie), so irrepressibly bubbly I suspect she may have been born carbonated, was there to help settle me into my charming accommodation. There were fully screened windows all around, and a second shower under the stars if that took my fancy, although it was a tad cold for an outdoor

The rhino that chased me up an acacia tree seconds after I took this photograph

Some believe the bateleur to be a spirit messenger

Sometimes elephant eyes take on the colour of the ocean

A typical view through the windscreen of my 4x4

With the documentary film crew around Mpofu pan

Revelling in the close company of Misty

Contemplating life with the W family

Minister Francis Nhema (front seat) and Darlington Duwa (head of Forestry Commission) with Misty and me

John Foster with the mounted baboon spider that he presented to me

The hippo that glared at me with his nostrils flared

Teaching others about the Presidential Elephants

© Mark Stratton

© Natural History Unit Africa

*With Minister Francis Nhema the day before the Presidential decree
reaffirmation ceremony*

Two species at one with each other

At the decree reaffirmation ceremony at Ganda Lodge, holding the document signed by President Robert Mugabe

Willa and family

Willa and I shared an intimate interlude before I kissed her

wash in May. Shayne warned that a hot-water bottle would be placed in my wide, comfy-looking bed each evening to take the edge off the chilly nights, just in case I mistook it for an alarming, warm-blooded beastie and thought it prudent to club it to death. Then she opened the door to the toilet, a small room with a great view, and said simply, 'No reading matter provided. None required.'

A little later, as I sat there with my undies around my ankles, I was startled by a red-billed francolin and her five tiny chicks, scuttling straight towards me. I could also see an elephant bull wandering away from the pan, hoping that he couldn't see me.

That afternoon I joined guests from Seattle, who were revelling in their very first trip to wild Africa. They'd seen a leopard lounging in a tree right by the roadside that very morning, and now their eyes searched feverishly among the branches of every tree, within beautiful groves of umtshibi and leadwood, in the hope of another sighting. Sunset was spectacular with elephants, giraffes, zebras, elands and the haunting cries of jackals the perfect accompaniment to our refreshing G&Ts.

Wilderness know how to take you on a game drive. Not one that I went on – and there are always two on offer each day – lasted for less than four hours. What's more, they consciously keep the number of vehicles at each sighting to a welcome minimum, for humans and wildlife alike.

That night, after a lively and tasty meal, I was escorted to my tent and found there, rolled neatly and placed at the end of my bed, a story. Africa is all about stories and this was an ingenious touch. I climbed into bed and unravelled the scroll of white paper. The narrative posed an interesting question: 'Who is the *real* king of the African jungle?' The smug lion demanded an answer from a towering elephant, who proceeded to sweep the lion off his feet with its powerful trunk, and throw him against tree and then against rock. 'You don't have to be so nasty and violent, just because you don't know the answer,' was the lion's immodest response! The elephant positively won that one. I liked that story, of course.

Snuggled up with the cosy hot-water bottle I soon dozed off, but awoke with a start when I heard a leopard calling, prowling close to my tent. And then there was the most dreadful, prolonged bellowing from a buffalo. A jumble of hooves broke the water in the pan, and then thundered off away from camp. I jumped out of bed and stood outside, my eyes darting around, but it was too dark to piece the story together. Believing that this incident would likely remain a secret of the African night, I climbed back into bed and fell into a deep sleep, waking before dawn to the pleasant, persistent call of a pearl-spotted owl.

'It sounded like that buffalo had a lion on its back,' I declared at our early breakfast meet.

'That was a buffalo?' queried one of the Americans in disbelief.

We all agreed that it was a buffalo in serious distress. As it turned out, during the course of our morning game drive, it wasn't in fact a lion that had been on that poor buffalo's back. It was a hyena. The buffalo had taken refuge in the middle of a nearby pan, with four loping hyenas at its edges. The poor old boy had no tail. The hyenas eventually took to the bushes, and we left too, before the buffalo regained enough confidence to risk a dash to safety. It was only the next day, when we saw the buffalo again at a different pan, that the full extent of his injuries was evident. He was a doomed dugga boy. Not only had he lost his tail, he had lost his manhood as well. These were incredibly bold, and skilled, hyenas. Sibs told us a story about a pack of eight that had previously brought down a buffalo, right by the camp lounge, and later dragged it across the floor, and dined on it beside the bar.

I was particularly keen to visit a part of the Wilderness concession that I love – Mbiza, where lala palm-fringed plains exude a decidedly spiritual aura. It's a stunning place at sunset and not at all what you expect to find in Hwange. Lewis guided us there, expertly as always. 'My little Hawaii,' he declared.

We were a safari vehicle full of guests getting along like wildfire and determined to have a great time. Shaynie managed to escape work for a few hours and climbed on-board with us. The scenery was awesome, the sunset and full-moonrise were breathtaking, the company, drinks and nibbles especially pleasant, but apart from a few ostriches and zebras, the wildlife was in hiding. None of us had a single regret, though. We packed up our beverage glasses and sundowner table and climbed back on-board our 4x4, rugging ourselves up in preparation for the arctic night-drive home.

'Hold on, I need to pee,' I cried, jumping off to squat behind the vehicle. I had only just climbed back on ...

'Lions!' Shaynie yelped.

'Yea, right Shaynie,' I thought to myself, while letting out a murmur of disbelief. By now I was very used to the never-ending jokes about what was about to eat you.

'No, man, really! Lions, right there,' she blurted out, letting the spotlight guide the way.

'Oh shit,' I squawked, swallowing my distrust. 'Those lions just watched me pee.'

'I bet that makes you want to pee again,' giggled one of the Americans beside me.

Four regal lions, relaxing right in front of us, under a full moon. They bellowed. Hyenas howled. It was glorious. Even Shaynie seemed relaxed – mind you, that was more likely the extra tot of gin that I'd slipped into her G&T.

Lewis always walked around with a smile, and a stick. It was a bit like a broom stick.

'Lewis wouldn't be Lewis without his stick,' grinned Sibs.

'What does he do with his stick?' I asked.

'You'll see,' was all that Sibs offered, with a deliberate air of mystery.

We did soon see. Lewis pulled up one morning where a leopard had taken a nap on the road – when there's no leopard, looking at its spoor and where it rested is the next best thing – and he took out his stick and poked around in leopard pee.

Like seemingly all of the Wilderness staff, Lewis likes abbreviations. He pointed out BBJs and LBRs – black-backed jackals and lilac-breasted rollers – and Zazu (from *The Lion King*), who is a red-billed hornbill. Lewis intrigued me. I wanted to know more and his story turned out to be an incredible one.

Lewis is one of five siblings. He lost both of his parents, who were in line for chieftaincy, when he was 12 years old. They were poisoned in order to fast-track another family's rise in the community. This brought an end to his education. He became a street kid, living out of 'the white man's garbage bins in Harare' for four long years. In these same bins he found discarded books and pens. He read, 'borrowed' a few words here and there, and wrote and sold poetry on the streets to help keep himself alive. Now, here he is. He's been a safari guide for 14 years. And he's great at it. He's knowledgeable, he's animated and he's convivial. He's Lewis, with his stick. It's that African magic, with a touch of fairy dust, that keeps one marvelling at what can be.

Marvel I did again during my final day at Little Mak, and still today I'm blown away recollecting such an amazing spectacle. Guides with 25 years' experience had never encountered such a thing and certainly Lewis hadn't either.

In less than a kilometre – an impossibly short distance in the wild, where the big cat species typically go out of their way to avoid each other – there were three cheetah cubs on a termite mound by the roadside, a little further on in the low branches of a tree there were two leopards on an impala kill and then, just around the corner, there were seven lions. Earlier, we had jokingly prayed to the patron saint of pussy cats, but this was astonishing! Stumbling upon cheetahs, leopards and lions so close together was incredibly special indeed.

The seven lions lazed about on the road, completely at ease with our close presence. They were all cubs, of varying sizes, from the known Ngamo pride. Their four mums, and dad, were apparently off hunting. Well, perhaps dad wasn't hunting; he was more likely supervising. Lewis took us to try to find them. We eventually ran into one of the mums, heading back, empty-handed (or was that empty-pawed?), towards the cubs. Then, after the moon had risen round and gorgeous, we came upon the other three, along with dad, as magnificent as can be. Dad's name is Cecil. 'Why would the lion researchers call such a magnificent beast Cecil?' I wondered to myself with a frown. It seemed like such a non-masculine name. Then Lewis began to speak of Cecil John Rhodes, the founder of Rhodesia (renamed Zimbabwe at Independence). He still didn't look like a Cecil to me; he was huge, powerfully built and majestic, clearly with a love of women. I decided, as he bellowed unforgettably to the full moon and the myriad stars above, that I would, instead, always think of him as Astro, astronomical in more ways than one. It was an absolute pleasure to be on safari here.

The word 'safari' is actually Swahili for 'journey'. Wilderness' motto is: 'Our journeys change people's lives.' I could believe it. The Little Makalolo guestbook is full of high praise, with recurring words like 'paradise', 'pure pleasure' and 'perfection'; 'spectacular', 'sensational' and 'superb'. Repeat guests are common. They are doing it right.

From Little Makalolo I transferred to Davison's Camp – named after Ted Davison, the first Hwange warden – where more than 50 elephants materialised from the bush to greet me. There are nine luxury tents, with uninterrupted views over a large pan, and a more rustic feel. Here too was Dixon, another ex-Hwange Estate guide. I was once again among old friends.

I was staying at Davison's for just one night. My time here was all too short but I knew that fun with Shaynie and my fellow American and European guests would continue on, long into the night. It was here that I was introduced to the novel concept of the Ugly Five. In all of my time in Africa I'd never heard of this and I found the idea rather unfortunate. I could certainly understand Marabou storks being on this list; that's one ugly bird. But hyena and wildebeest? Well, I thought, perhaps that is a fair assessment. Warthog and hippo, though? That's downright undeserved!

The Linkwasha concession, which houses Davison's camp and was also the setting of our big-cat encounter, is frequently packed with wildlife. One afternoon we encountered 11 species in about as many minutes: elephant, waterbuck, impala, zebra, ostrich, wildebeest, giraffe, buffalo, hippo, baboon and jackal. It's certainly a memorable place of the wild.

We sat down for dinner that night, with Dixon at the head of the table, and Shaynie seated beside me. The menu was announced, with dessert 'a surprise'. 'A surprise,' I repeated with a smile, suspecting nothing untoward.

My fellow guests from overseas had a keen interest in elephants and I found myself having to stop answering their enthusiastic questions so that I could finish my meal. Shaynie disappeared for a few minutes, on request from a staff member, but still I suspected nothing.

Soon, dessert arrived, and with it: 'Happy birthday to you … Happy birthday to you.' It wasn't my birthday. My birthday had passed a couple of weeks earlier and, besides, it had been my 49th birthday and one that I really didn't need to be reminded about. An iced cake and a bottle of champagne were ceremoniously placed in front of me. I was immediately suspicious of the lump of cake.

'Shaynie!' I cried, struggling to find appropriate words. 'I've worked with elephants for ten years and this looks exceptionally dubious!'

Shaynie just sat there, trying to look completely innocent. Everyone around the table was clearly in on this, and the laughter and frivolity was being enjoyed by all.

'Look,' Shaynie said to me, poking her finger into the icing, and licking it off extravagantly. 'There's nothing wrong with it.'

I sat there, mouth partially open and shaking my head, knowing exactly what was in front of me. I'd seen 'deposits' of this size and shape thousands of times before.

'The chef spent hours baking you this cake. You seem a bit ungrateful,' lamented Shaynie.

'If this is the quality of cake that your chef makes, then maybe you need to think about getting yourself a new chef,' I joked. Meanwhile, I'd stuck the knife into the iced heap in front of me, nearly snapping off its tip in the process.

'If I cut this Shaynie, do you promise, on your mother's life, to eat a piece?'

Shaynie was quiet. Amid more laughter, I broke open the expertly iced ball of dried elephant dung.

'Hhhhmmm,' I sighed, taking in a good whiff. 'It smells like elephant.'

The real cake eventually made it to the table, and we raised our glasses in a champagne toast, to the elephants, and enjoyed a slice of freshly baked, moist chocolate cake, with not a smidgen of pachyderm poo in sight.

As I packed up to leave the next morning, I reflected on Wilderness Safaris' impressive conservation record. Their Wildlife Trust is an extension of their safari business and this focus isn't a publicity stunt, as it can indeed appear to be for some others. They employ a full-time wildlife co-ordinator in Hwange, and are actively involved with an assortment of conservation initiatives: anti-poaching, game water and educational programs for children. There were times when it had actually made me sad being on the Wilderness concessions, because this is what the Hwange Estate *used* to look like. Wilderness were thoughtfully supplying plentiful water for their abundant wildlife – in fact they were already pumping 14 pans early in the dry season.

I said my thank yous and goodbyes to Courteney, one of the Wilderness directors. 'Thank you for all you do for Hwange conservation,' he said to me in return.

If only he knew how much I wanted to put him in my duffel bag and take him with me. I recognised, as another wave of longing washed over me, what someone like him, and his company, could do for the Presidential Elephants and the land on which they roam. But alas, this inspired Wilderness group operates outside their key home range.

The film crew and
more crazy carry-on

In July 2011 those damn dragons were back yet again. The Dete police were on my case, once more, this time following up on an alleged complaint from Hwange Safari Lodge – which was still being leased by African Sun – that I was *sabotaging* their business.

I'd had nothing whatsoever to do with this group since they controversially evicted me ten months earlier, and I certainly had no desire to do so, yet I was supposedly single-handedly succeeding in sabotaging their business. My perceived capabilities and purported deeds were mind-boggling, and starting to surprise even me! In my opinion, African Sun didn't need any help from me, or from anyone else. They had already done, and were apparently still doing, a fine job of sabotaging themselves.

Press reports at the time stated that African Sun had lost leases on hotels in South Africa after they couldn't meet lease obligations, although their own press statements claimed they'd chosen to break these leases. It was also looking likely that they might lose leases on some of their properties within Zimbabwe too, perhaps even on the Hwange Safari Lodge itself, which must have had them feeling rather desperate.

The saboteur accusation was so ridiculous that I decided not to waste time defending myself. Naturally enough, when asked by the police, they weren't able to provide proof to back this latest claim. Even their contacts in the Dete police force, and various other agencies, saw through them in the end. It helped that I still had a copy of the 'partnership agreement' they served on me, which I was happy to share with bemused others on request. (The rondavel that I'd lived in for nine years still lay vacant, so they obviously hadn't found anybody else willing to live in it.)

It seemed, though, that they might now resort to anything to get me out of the area permanently. It must have been humiliating for them that I should return to Hwange, moving forward stronger than ever.

After more days, that turned into weeks, of investigations and questions and demands that I was never going to agree to, everyone finally backed off and I was left to continue with my day-to-day activities in relative peace. It was surely time for the police to realise that they were continually wasting their time, and mine, investigating the wrong person. I suggested to them, in no uncertain terms, that they should concentrate their investigations on those who report me. Then, perhaps, they might actually find the bad guys.

What was most astonishing about this latest carry-on was that I now had a five-person film crew with me who were privy to all of this. The filming of the documentary on my life and my work with the Presidential Elephants was now underway and must have gotten under African Sun's skin. They had only themselves to blame for ruining their chances of benefiting significantly from this documentary, and they were now clearly attempting to ensure that nobody else benefited either. The latest accusations certainly hadn't worked to their advantage, but did allow the film crew a first-hand glimpse into the sort of senseless issues that regularly hamper my work in Zimbabwe.

The crew had successfully reapplied to the appropriate Zimbabwean authorities for their filming permits, after their previous ones had lapsed while I was finding somewhere new to live, and filming had begun in earnest. Although African Sun still had me banned from the State Land area of Kanondo, the Parks Authority and the Environment Ministry were fortunately not easily blindsided by them. They stepped in, dictating that no one could stop my monitoring of the Presidential Elephants on any land on which they roam, so long as I was accompanied by a Parks Authority scout when I travelled into areas where local approvals weren't in place. So that's exactly what I did, but I did it only rarely. Since elephants wander over considerable distances there were, naturally enough, other areas where I could monitor the Presidential Elephants, and I now chose to spend as much time away from the Hwange Safari Lodge/Kanondo area as possible. Visiting the area left me with a feeling of distaste, although I knew that I would still have to monitor family groups there whenever the need arose.

I always knew that the Presidential Elephants wandered in the adjoining Forestry Commission/Ganda Lodge area but I hadn't spent much time there to date. Now, with a new agreement with Forestry in place, I started frequenting these areas, and delighted in what I saw. There were six attractive waterholes that enticed hordes of elephants. I came across family after family of Presidential Elephants. It felt like I'd been reborn.

The change of scenery was also revitalising. There were attractive jackal-berry trees (the purplish round fruit is often eaten by jackals, hence the common name) beside many of the waterholes, which are not frequently seen elsewhere. The elephants devour Scotsman's rattle pods (straight, woody-brown pods used as rattles by the locals) while in these areas, rather than acacia pods. The pan in front of Ganda Lodge is regularly peppered with waterbuck, impalas, kudus, zebras and warthogs. As I stood chatting to the Ganda Lodge manager one afternoon, a lioness snatched one of the warthogs right before our eyes.

Out of bad, I've learnt, there always comes something good, eventually, and a new relationship was forged with the Forestry Commission and its Ganda Lodge. What's more, it transpired that African Sun didn't actually own the portion of Presidential Elephant land that they claimed to. Dawn Properties turned out to be the actual owners of a large portion of the Hwange Estate. This included the areas around Foster's pan, Mtaka pan and Mpofu pan, which are situated conveniently close to where I live at Miombo Safari Camp, as well as around the Safari Lodge sewerage plant, which is also frequented by the elephants. Dawn Properties granted me full authority to continue working with the Presidential Elephants in these areas.

African Sun seemed to be losing round after round and it was becoming clear to many that all of their carry-on had backfired. This broken relationship was one thing that I had no desire to try to rebuild.

* * * * *

I really wasn't sure how I'd cope having a film crew with me every day for several months, as I continued my work with the Presidential Elephants on the Forestry Commission/Ganda Lodge and Dawn Properties land areas. As accustomed as I was to leading a relatively solitary bush life, the filming seemed like a big imposition at first. I had only met Kira, the documentary producer, briefly once before when she was documenting the release into Hwange National Park of some formerly-abused elephants. She'd cornered me one evening and asked to interview me on camera. Now, two years later, here we were.

Kira worked for Triosphere in South Africa who'd been commissioned by Natural History Unit Africa to produce this documentary. The concept of an international documentary certainly fitted well with my mission to increase awareness of the Presidential Elephants, and their ongoing battles. Although I wasn't sure I was ready for it, I knew that it could do the elephants a great deal of good, and might also raise my own profile enough to force some of the annoying individuals in the area off my back. But then again, it could have the opposite effect. This was Zimbabwe, and you just never knew how some might react. But, if I could entice a wider audience to fall in love with these elephants, just as I had with many others, then their ongoing safety and survival would be more assured. There could, of course, be no pre-prepared script to work to in such a wild environment, and how the footage was edited was entirely out of my hands. Given how some of the media loved to try to portray Zimbabwe in a particularly negative light, I had obtained assurances that the output would in no way be manipulated to compromise Zimbabwe or my ongoing work with the elephants, and I had to trust that these promises held true. After weighing everything up, there seemed to be more pros than cons, and I had agreed to proceed.

Along with Kira, there was Richard the director, and (in different combinations over the weeks that followed) Riaan, Dale, Don, JJ and Andre, who were the camera and sound men. They were all accommodated at Miombo Safari Camp. 'You'd better hope that you get on with them,' was the sort of sentiment I heard repeatedly from friends before the crew arrived, knowing that this wasn't just a short stay. Many imagined that the whole process might drive me insane. Fortunately, everything worked out just fine.

Film crews are always going to push the boundaries for a great shot, though, and I was constantly on the lookout to ensure that they never pushed them too far. They knew that I wasn't kidding when I said something like, 'I don't particularly care if the elephants kill you if you're doing something stupid. But if *they* get killed because they've killed you, then I care.' They were a very professional bunch and only very occasionally did I need to intervene. Mostly, over our many weeks together in the field, there were a lot of laughs and frivolity to be had. First, though, there was some serious filming to be done.

* * * * *

Minister Francis Nhema, from the Ministry of the Environment and Natural Resources, had agreed to make public on film the reaffirmation of the Presidential decree, on behalf of President Mugabe. I painstakingly organised a small function at Ganda Lodge, where the minister and his delegation would stay for one night. It would be attended only by those who had shown support for the Presidential Elephants: representatives from the Forestry Commission, Dawn Properties, the Parks Authority and the President's office, as well as a few supportive colleagues from the research and photographic-safari communities. Chief Nelukoba Dingani (who is the area's traditional leader, akin to a tribal king) would also be in attendance, as would representatives from the media. Ingonyama, an exceptionally talented local dance and drama group from Dete, would be there to help welcome the minister and the chief. The Forestry Protection Unit, who is involved in snare destruction in the Presidential Elephants' key home range, would be there to present themselves to the minister for official inspection.

I just knew something would go wrong. Something always goes wrong. This was Zimbabwe after all. Just two days before the function I found myself at Ganda Lodge, where preparations were well underway, talking to Minister Nhema on my mobile.

'Air Zimbabwe's just gone on strike. I can't make it to Hwange,' the minister said to me.

No, no, no, no, NO! I simply wasn't going to let this happen. We spoke calmly about various options but none were doable or acceptable, at least not to me.

'What if we can charter a plane for you?' I offered as a last resort, not knowing if I could pull this off.

'That would be okay,' he said.

I asked him to give me half an hour. I hung up, feeling faint. We had half an hour to get approvals to pay for this flight, to see if a suitable plane was even available to fly from Harare into the Hwange airport, and to get a schedule organised. Half an hour later I rang the minister back. Everything was in place; he just had to get himself to the airport.

That half an hour of controlled chaos actually came with an upside. We could now request to film the minister's flight arrival on the Hwange tarmac, although this in itself proved to be yet another mission. It certainly didn't happen quickly, or easily, but the film crew were finally granted the approvals they needed.

The minister arrived the morning before the official function. It was planned that I would take him out in my 4x4 after lunch, with film crew in tow, to meet some of the Presidential Elephants. It was unusually windy and cold and I feared the elephants would be in hiding. Thank goodness for the Ms and the Es. They were there waiting for us at Mutandasoka pan, just down the road from Ganda Lodge. Misty was beautiful as always, standing just centimetres from the door of my 4x4, as was Eileen and her family.

In my backseat was Darlington Duwa, the head of the Forestry Commission, who is a good friend of Minister Nhema's. He was initially terrified of the elephants being so close, and shuffled right over beside the cameraman on the other side of the seat. The next minute he had become so enthralled with this encounter that he couldn't get enough of them, clicking away with the camera on his mobile phone. We were on Forestry land after all, and he had every reason to feel enthusiastic and proud.

Minister Nhema was standing on the passenger seat, up through the roof of my 4x4, gazing into Misty's eye, visibly astonished. He too had never before met the Presidential Elephants. 'Amazing!' he eventually said, flashing an impressive smile while turning towards me. 'So that's why you sing "Amazing Grace" to them.'

I do sing 'Amazing Grace' to them. Even with my terrible voice, it was visibly calming to them in dreadful days past. But I wasn't about to sing to them now. This day belonged to the minister.

Back at Ganda Lodge late that afternoon, Minister Nhema recounted his experiences to the Forestry Commission staff who had gathered to greet him on his return. I couldn't understand what was being said but there were wide eyes and lots of laughter and broad smiles at his digital-camera screen. Apparently the minister spoke excitedly about his time with the Presidential Elephants right throughout the evening, and I couldn't help but smile with delight.

The official function the next morning went off without a hitch. Minister Nhema passed on wishes and congratulations from President Mugabe. He spoke to the attentive audience about families, in the context of *elephant* families. He spoke of families more organised, with more love, respect and better attitude, and less greed and selfishness, than human families. He concluded that the wilderness was more civilised than what we call civilisation, and said that the world could learn a lot more from the Presidential Elephants than it could from elsewhere. He shared with everyone the fact that his eyes had been opened to a world of love and respect, as reflected in the Presidential Elephants. I have often been asked why I would choose another species over my own, and the minister had explained it admirably. My love and understanding and awe of the elephants had spilled over to him. The Presidential decree reaffirmation was then read and applauded.

Chief Dingani spoke too. Towards the end of his speech, everyone erupted into laughter. Still with no grasp of the complicated isiNdebele language, I didn't know what was going on. Someone beside me whispered a translation. The chief was going to find me a husband! The minister seemed to find this particularly amusing, while I chortled along too, hoping this would quickly be forgotten. I'm told, though, that it was an honour.

It had been a humbling few days for me. I was overwhelmed by the gracious words and camaraderie, despite knowing that it might not last. Over the years I'd frequently felt that I was the only one who truly cared about these elephants. But now, I dared to hope, if ever there was another battle to save the Presidential Elephants, I wouldn't be alone.

A week later, Minister Nhema was quoted in a newspaper article saying:

Anyone who shoots at the Presidential herd is as bad as someone shooting at the president. When you shoot at these animals, you can expect to be shot back at. If you kill them, you will also be killed. No one should compromise the Presidential herd.

And I felt a warm glow, deep in my heart.

* * * * *

The decree celebration was over and it was time for us to get on with elephant-specific filming. As it turned out, there were plenty of memorable, and amusing, moments with the crew. By the time filming was complete we'd had many close encounters with the adorable Courtney, Cathy and other members of the C family, but this was early days and the crew were still feeling their way. We were standing around our vehicles one day, in the shade of a leafy tree, eating lunch.

'Sharon!' cried JJ, with an audible sense of urgency. I looked around. He was peering at me out of the corner of his eyes. 'Is this safe?' he asked, barely moving his lips. JJ was standing beside one of the vehicles, a big, grey, fluffy microphone in his hand. Courtney and family had digressed from their path and were now lumbering straight towards him. It was definitely less safe to tell him to move now and so, although I didn't particularly like what I saw, I said simply, 'It's fine. Just don't move. Stay right beside the vehicle.'

Eyes wide, holding his breath, JJ didn't move a muscle. Courtney's massive grey body passed within touching distance of him. His eyes still bulging, JJ let out a huge sigh of relief. He'd had his first 'code brown' moment, and everyone laughed nervously, their own hearts racing in support. Others, I suspect, were also close to needing a clean pair of pants.

Later on, Andre nearly lost his big, fluffy mic to an inquisitive male, and later still, with Riaan in tow, had his own 'code brown' moment with a disgruntled Courtney. 'Good girl, Courtney,' I said aloud. 'You show these boys who's boss.'

There was always an assortment of tasks on the filming schedule that had to be completed, so we typically didn't leave for the pan areas for elephant filming until after 10 a.m. each day. I knew from experience that few elephants would be out and about before then anyway. After Riaan attached one of his small cameras to a short, wooden rod and manoeuvred it only centimetres away from huge, grey faces and trunks and bodies, without so much as a flinch from some of my favourite elephant friends, he shook his head and announced with a grin, gesturing towards me, 'Now I know why we don't come out earlier. Sharon only lets them out of their cages at 10 a.m.!'

Some of the very well-known Presidential Elephants were proving to be unbelievably tolerant. It was going to be tough to convince the world that every second of this footage was filmed with wild, free-roaming elephants. There were times, like when a camera actually touched an eyelash, that even I shook my head in disbelief. It was members of the C family – most notably Courtney and her adult son Court – who were impossibly relaxed around the cameras. Members of the W family – Whole, Willa, Whosit and Wilma – came a close second. Sometimes I'd look on with nerves starting to mount. 'Okay. Don't push your luck. It's time for me to chain them back up now,' I'd kid.

Whenever there's a blooper segment on a movie DVD, I usually make a point of watching it. Laughing at other people's misfortune and mistakes is highly entertaining. During the daily filming I got to laugh at such things first-hand, and I was generally laughing at myself.

One afternoon, with elephants all around and drink in hand, Kira was firing questions at me. I don't remember what the particular question was, but all of a sudden, after taking a sip of my drink, there was something very alien in my mouth. Without a hint of grace I involuntarily spat the liquid, along with the alien being, back into the glass and there, wriggling around, was a slimy yellow-and-red grub with tiny spikes. 'Oh, gross, I just had a *grub* in my mouth,' I cried, looking down with a shudder into the glass. Plah! Plah! I was rubbing my tongue along my teeth and flicking it out of my mouth. 'Yuk! Yuk, YUK!' I wasn't parked under any trees and couldn't work out how the grub had suddenly turned up in my glass in the first place. Elephants were shaking their heads right beside me, so perhaps it had flown off a huge, grey ear. Soon I was in a fit of laughter. My tongue was tingling. 'Does the red mean this grub's poisonous? My tongue's going numb,' I blurted.

No one answered. Everyone was too busy laughing, at my expense, with not a smidgen of sympathy, and hinted that I shouldn't be such a city girl. Riaan had earlier teased me in the same vein when I'd been whining about how he shouldn't be filming my fingernails in close up when they were so unbelievably dirty, and the same went for my feet.

I guess there is still some city girl in me and perhaps I am something of an enigma. Andrea, one of my New Zealand girlfriends, still can't reconcile my current self with the one she regularly travelled with overseas on business, when I would worry about *everything*: whether the airline would lose our bags, whether the next hotel would have our booking, whether the alarm clock was set properly for the morning or whether we were adequately prepared for our next meeting. But worry about poisonous grubs and dirty fingernails and feet, not to mention the possibility of being flattened by a huge hippo or devoured by a hungry lion? Never!

I gazed back at the grub that was now sitting on my outstretched finger. Australian aboriginals might eat witchetty grubs, just like many Africans eat mopane worms, but I had absolutely no desire to join them in these types of delicacies. 'If I wake up dead in the morning, you'll know it was poisonous,' I frowned.

I have become convinced that sound guys only become sound guys so that they can put their hands down women's tops. JJ and I had an early morning ritual that usually resulted in a laugh initially, and later in a smirk and a mock-loving embrace. Every morning, he needed to attach a microphone to me and the best place for it, given that I'm not one to try to look like Jane of the jungle and just wear a black stretchy top under a throw-shirt when in the field, was on the inside of my top, right between my boobs (a bra, incidentally, hasn't been part of my wardrobe for the past ten years). It was a little awkward for everyone, the first few times, but having his hands down my top soon became a normal occurrence. When JJ left and Riaan took over the role of both cameraman and sound guy, Riaan and I shared these same cosy moments. But when Riaan headed off elsewhere I decided that enough was enough. There would be no more strange men with their hands down my top, and I learnt to secure the microphone myself.

What I loathed most was the large battery pack, attached to the microphone with a rather thick cable, which had to be secured to the band of my skirt. It was too uncomfortable to attach to the back of my skirt given that I was sitting for much of the time and it dug into the small of my back. So, most often I attached it to my side, which added a good few centimetres to my girth, but by now I was past caring.

Although the crew had hired two vehicles from Frogs Safaris to film from, there was one memorable day when I had an extra three people in my 4x4: Kira, Richard and JJ. Kira is petite and, too frequently for her own comfort, she found herself squashed in the footwell of my passenger seat when we came across a family of elephants unexpectedly. The cameras had to roll, and Kira wasn't supposed to be there. I'm sure her voice was picked up on the microphones many times, cursing in the footwell.

So, when we ran into the W family out of the blue, and all three had to quickly disappear from sight, Kira was once again in the footwell, JJ and all of his sound gear was sprawled across the back seat, and Richard was lying awkwardly in the rear, squashed alongside a tin trunk and all of our many lunch boxes. There were groans of discomfort and W family elephants peering in through the windows at this unusual phenomenon.

When the shoot was over, Richard popped up from the back, still moaning. Whosit was very close to where he now sat, her face on one side of the glass and Richard's on the other. Her look was one of incredulous wonder. She tilted her head to one side. 'What the fuck are you doing in there?' was precisely what I imagined her saying to him.

On another day Riaan and Richard were together inside my vehicle. Riaan started to film, so Richard had to disappear from frame. When I looked around he was leaning way out through one of the rear windows. Misty appeared right beside him and suddenly they were head to head. Misty is too much of a lady to use the 'f' word, but I heard in my mind more mystified sentiments, '*Forgodsake* man. What on earth are you *doing*?'

On Dale's first day in the field, when the elephants were already very used to the film crew vehicles, and especially relaxed when my 4x4 was right there too, he stood behind his camera and simply shook his head. Some W family members were just centimetres away, and even his wide-angle lens wasn't wide enough. He was perfectly at ease, just clearly mystified by what he'd come to film. For a few seconds his expression was one of sheer disbelief. When I feared that the inquisitive Whosit was about to climb on the back of his open vehicle with him, and with one flick of a trunk there could have been trouble, I instructed his driver to move off.

On another day Dale was trying to film Wish and Wishful. I was becoming increasingly concerned about little Wish, son of Whosit, because he simply wasn't growing as he should be and we were endeavouring to get some footage to show their difference in size. Suddenly, quick as a flash, there was a W family trunk inside my back window, grabbing at a bright-yellow jacket that I carried to slip on in the cold winter evenings. The elephant grabbed one sleeve and I instinctively grabbed the other. A tug of war ensued, me pulling on one end and the elephant pulling on the other. Back and forth, back and forth, the jacket was see-sawing through the window. I was mic'd up, as always – I couldn't even burp without being heard – and Dale quickly turned his camera my way when he picked up my cursing through his earphones.

Thinking that my jacket was about to be ripped in two, and realising that this determined elephant wasn't going to let go, I released my grip. She'd won, and she was unashamedly proud of herself. 'Hey! I certainly hope you plan to give that back,' I scolded. Other W family members ran towards her and a real commotion ensued at the sight of this bright-yellow object in her trunk. It was as if all of the elephants knew it was mine and thought this hilarious. If elephants giggle in infrasound then they were certainly giggling wildly now. Soon they all raced off into the bush, with my jacket in tow. 'Hey! Give me back my jacket,' I cried, but she had no intention of giving it back.

She suddenly tossed it over her head and the bright-yellow jacket flew through the air. They were all having a ball – at my expense! It was too overgrown for me to see what happened next and, as the cheeky grey monsters moved off, I wondered if I would ever see my jacket again. I did eventually retrieve the jacket, rather damp with elephant slobber but otherwise unharmed.

There are quite a few non-descript teenaged elephants in the extended W family, and on this day members of Whole's, Wilma's, Wide's, Wanda's and Wiona's immediate families had all been mingling together. Everything had happened in a flash and I hadn't positively identified who had stolen my jacket, although I was pretty sure it was one of Whole's family.

It was more than a week before we found ourselves back with Whole and her family. All of a sudden there was a trunk through my window and someone was pulling on my skirt. It was Winna. 'Hey!

You can't steal my skirt; I'm *wearing* this skirt,' I reprimanded. Then, with memories of the jacket incident flooding back, I looked at her quizzically and exclaimed, 'Hey Winna! Was it *you* who stole my jacket?'

It was less light-hearted on the day that I was racing through the bush at speed, responding to a snared-elephant sighting at Kanondo. One of the filming vehicles needed to rush to Main Camp to collect a Parks Authority scout. Kira was already in my 4x4, but now Dale with his camera gear and Andre with his sound gear were crammed in as well so as not to miss anything. The situation had unfolded so suddenly that all of this was unplanned, but Dale started to film and Andre to record. It's impossible to get to Main Camp and back quickly so we continued on without the scout. When it comes to snared animals there's no time to lose, since the chance of the elephant disappearing into thick bush is always high.

I had phoned Esther to dart the elephant, and now Hans, Esther's husband, was calling me on the radio. I could hear his voice but couldn't find my radio. It must have been dislodged when everyone clambered into my 4x4.

Riaan had started to film from the second crew vehicle and so my passengers were required to stay down and out of sight; it was an impossibly squashed state of affairs given the number of people and amount of equipment. I was feeling agitated, as I always seem to during snare removal attempts, and this one didn't look like it was going to succeed. Esther and Hans had been further away when they received my call and still had to return to their base to collect equipment, and then deal with a herd of elephants blocking their path. Time was running out. The snared elephant's family had been trying to move off for some time and were becoming more and more restless as I herded them back and forth, back and forth, doing my best to keep them in the open. It certainly looked like we were going to lose them.

Now it was me using the 'f' word, and in not a particularly friendly tone. 'Where the fuck is my radio?' I squawked from behind the steering wheel, feeling around and not able to put my hands on it. I could hear Hans's voice addressing me, but I couldn't find the radio. 'Will somebody please find my radio,' I swore. 'I *need* the goddamn radio. I have to be able to talk to Hans.'

Professionals as always, everyone stayed lying down and out of sight. Then silently, and rather spookily, a disembodied hand appeared beside me, clasping the radio. I felt like I was in a scene from *The Addams Family*.

This snare removal attempt wasn't successful, but a different one thankfully was. We didn't do much filming in the Kanondo area, given my ongoing problems with African Sun, but we went there one day to get footage of a huge *acacia erioloba* and to look for Lady. It wasn't long before we stumbled upon a family of National Park elephants that had a youngster with a tight snare around his front, left leg. The wire had not yet broken the skin, but the snare was awfully tight, with a long wire attached, and it would soon inflict serious injury. Tragically, it was too late in the afternoon to dart, so we returned the next day and fortunately found the family again. One phone call to Esther and Hans and they were immediately on their way to dart.

I had never known an elephant darting to be accomplished so quickly and smoothly. The elephant fell and Esther, Hans and I moved in. Both cameramen thought they had time to casually reposition themselves in order to get a better shot, but by the time they looked up Hans had used huge wire-cutters to remove the despicable four-wire snare. Somewhat mortified, they'd missed filming the crucial cutting of the wire! Cameras or no cameras, there's never any time to muck around. There were hundreds of elephants in the area and dangerous scenarios can materialise in a flash. Nobody was risking our normal protocols for the cameras.

Both Riaan and Dale were adventurous in the use of their camera equipment, and consequently there were dung-cams, water-cams, mineral-lick-cams and pole-cams, not to mention the cameras stuck to the inside of my windscreen to monitor my every move. I empathised with the elephants; there were times when I would have happily picked a camera up and thrown it away too. When the elephants did it, though, they were just having fun.

One day we were at Mutandasoka pan, close to Ganda Lodge. This pan, and the Dawn Properties' Mpofu pan that was ten kilometres away, had become our regular haunts. Riaan had expertly hollowed out the insides of a ball of elephant dung and placed a camera in the indent. He positioned it, surrounded by other dung balls to help disguise it, not far from the water's edge. It didn't take long before one young elephant started putting on a fine performance, right beside the camera. Then a bigger boy came along and promptly kicked the dung pile, exposing the camera. He picked the camera up and hurled it into the pan. I was secretly impressed. He was visibly chuffed with himself too. In fact I'm sure I saw him doing a celebratory two-step. 'Clever boy,' I whispered under my breath. The camera was eventually retrieved by one of the vehicle drivers who waded around in the murky, knee-deep water and smelly, muddy slop of the pan. And it was still rolling!

After that, I chose to stay close to the cameras. I didn't care about the camera, or the footage. I did worry, though, that one of the elephants might pick one up and swallow it.

'That'd be a great picture,' declared Riaan, forever the cameraman.

I glared at him. 'That's hardly the point,' I muttered.

All of these creative camera positions made for some great shots and a lot of laughs and I was happy for them to carry on, so long as no elephants ended up with a camera in their belly.

An undisguised friendly rivalry existed between the camera and sound specialists. Riaan's daily banter went something like this:

'Why does thunder come after lightning? – Even God has to wait for sound.'

'What's the difference between a soundman and a generator? – A generator stops whining when it's switched off after wrap'.

Then the fitting retort, 'What's the difference between a cameraman and God? – God doesn't think he's a cameraman.'

I couldn't help but think that this question was rather pertinent to my own situation:

'What's the difference between the corporate company that was trying to own me and God?'

Richard was keen for time-lapse footage of me sitting in a full-moonrise but there'd been terrible bushfires inside the national park, which had burnt all of the way to Botswana, and there was interminable smoke and haze across the horizon. On three occasions in the late afternoons, immediately preceding full moon, we were unable to even glimpse the moon until it was well up in the sky. Richard would have to settle for me in a sunset instead.

Dale set up his camera for a time-lapse shot while Kira, radio in hand, helped to position my vehicle in line with the setting sun and then strategically positioned me on my roof. They told me that I mustn't move for the next 45 minutes. I didn't appreciate how difficult this was until I was forced to do it. I had cramps in my legs and thought I might well slip down off the roof at any second. An eternity later I finally heard through my radio, 'Thank you!'

'Forgodsake! That better have been worth it,' I shouted with a laugh.

A 45 minute pose to get just 60 seconds of time-lapse footage! I looked at them sceptically while they assured me that the sunset was stunning and it had most definitely been worthwhile.

It was a regrettable fact that all of us, at one time or another, suffered from an upset stomach. Whether it was the food or the water we weren't sure, but something was certainly playing havoc with our insides on a regular basis. What the sound guys are forced to listen to through their earphones is unparalleled. On numerous occasions I'd be answering a question, blissfully unaware of the orchestral cacophony emanating from my digestive regions, when I'd be cut short, 'I can hear Sharon's stomach. Can we please do that again.' It got to the point where I'd stop myself, mid-sentence, and smirk towards the sound man, 'Cut? You're hearing my stomach in stereo, aren't you? Shall we do that again?' The day that it got so bad you couldn't distinguish between an elephant rumble and my stomach rumble, I lay down on the back seat of my 4x4 and slept.

Richard noticed a little wooden elephant in my 4x4, which had been carved for me many years previously. It once hung from my rear-view mirror but it'd been weakened by time and sunshine and now lay, a little forlorn, on its side on the dashboard. Someone decided, in all their wisdom, that it should be fixed to my bonnet. So it was, with glue that stuck fast.

For weeks I watched inquisitive elephants investigate this strange new object. Some put their trunk over it and sniffed, while others grabbed it with just enough pressure to lift it skyward, still partially attached by a string of glue. Unfortunately, the cameras were never in the right place at the right time.

It was glued and reglued. When it did finally disappear altogether, no one had a clue what had actually happened to it. Elephants all around my vehicle was a common occurrence and clearly everyone's attention had been focused somewhere else. I was a little sad about that wooden elephant and we searched the ground where we'd just spent time, but to no avail.

It did eventually turn up – well, half of it did at least – surrounded by elephant dung and partially buried in the ground. 'I think the other half is probably in an elephant's belly,' I lamented.

The crew knew that, since my return to Hwange, I hadn't yet met up with Lady and her family and they were keen to be there when I did. It was now 11 months since I'd seen this favourite family, which was by far the longest period of time away from them in over a decade.

We had just had lunch under a shady tree at Mutandasoka pan, close to Ganda Lodge. It was only Riaan and me, plus the driver of the crew vehicle and a Forestry scout. That morning Riaan had mounted a camera below the driver's-side door of my vehicle and warned me to travel slowly when it was attached. He'd removed it when we stopped for lunch. Now I was seated in my 4x4 asking Riaan if he wanted to reattach the camera. He decided to do just that. He was lying on his back, under my vehicle, when I saw her approaching the pan.

'It's Lady! ... Is it Lady? ... There's Lesley, and Lucky ... Yes! It's Lady. Riaan, I have to go!'

'Well you can't go yet,' retorted Riaan. 'I'm only half done.'

'Riaan, it's Lady! I have to go.'

'I can't do this any faster. What do you want me to do?'

I started my engine.

'If you don't get away from my wheel, I'll be forced to run right over the top of you,' I threatened.

I grabbed my binoculars to give Riaan a chance to finish. I could see that Lady and her family were muddy and had obviously already been to another pan before they arrived at this one. They wouldn't stay here for long. Soon they would disappear into thick bush.

'Riaan! I've got to go.'

He finished frantically and jumped away from my 4x4. Within seconds he was on the crew vehicle filming me.

By now I was feeling very emotional and just needed to get to her. I roared off, completely forgetting that I was supposed to travel slowly when this under-the-vehicle camera was attached. After a few hundred metres I stopped and called to Lady. She responded immediately. With the camera under my vehicle rolling, and Riaan racing to get to me with his professional gear, Lady came and greeted me for the first time in almost a year. It was a beautiful, poignant moment. 'My girl. Hey my girl,' I crooned.

After taking my fingers in the fingers of her trunk, Lady put her trunk on top of my head, and then over my mouth and nose in an elephant kiss! I'm still not sure what the cameras picked up, and right then I didn't care. Lady was fine. Her family was fine. And there was Lol, with a little baby boy beside her.

* * * * *

The filming, and the attention that it was drawing to the plight of the elephants, forced African Sun to finally reconnect municipal water to Mpofu pan. The water level had been looking dire, and elephant activity was increasing, so it wouldn't be long before it was bone dry. I approached Dawn Properties, who lease the land to African Sun, and explained the situation, stressing what the water meant to the wildlife and to the Presidential Elephants. I asked them to apply pressure to African Sun to be *responsible* tenants and within just a few days life-giving water was flowing. But Mtaka pan remained as dry as a bone.

* * * * *

The days and months flew by. I hadn't found time to wash my sheets or towels for weeks. The baboons had been playing havoc with my thatched roof, which meant that I'd had to arrange for a new layer of thatch at the front of my cottage. Thatching is such a messy job. My home was in disarray. I started texting friends, on a final countdown, 'Only five more sleeps to go, and I'm freeeeee!' … 'Only four more sleeps to go …'

The last day of filming finally came, and it was quite a few weeks earlier than had originally been planned. There was already some 200 hours of footage to somehow be cut into a 52-minute story (one hour, with ad breaks). Less than half of one per cent of the footage would make it into the documentary. The rest would end up on the cutting-room floor. No more footage was needed. The crew had already filmed some pretty remarkable stuff. I just hoped that they would take the time needed to unearth the best footage and successfully weave it into a great documentary.

The last piece to be shot was, bizarrely, a cheesecake-making get-together with my friend Laurie, who's associated with the Lion Research Project. We'd previously savoured the results of a packet cheesecake and a packet cappuccino under the shady trees in my front yard and I'd invited her over to do it again.

I met Laurie at my tall iron gate and we downed a glass of wine to help get us through this final filming. It was just a bit of fun.

It was around 2 p.m. on that Thursday, with another wine under my belt, when Kira finally declared with a smile and a tangible sense of achievement, 'Okay everybody, it's a wrap!'

Bend-down in Bulawayo

Bulawayo is a three-hour drive away and has become my escape from the bush whenever I feel the need for a dose of civilisation and some pizza and ice-cream. It's where I go to buy supplies, and whenever I visit I stay in the spare room in Shaynie's flat in town where I always feel at home. It is indeed my home away from home.

Barbara and her daughter Dee live next door, with Frank the landlord downstairs and an assortment of single folk who have come and gone over the years. It's a cosy little crowd where everyone looks out for one another. Shaynie's sister, CJ, comes into town occasionally and many a time we've found ourselves all sitting together on the outside staircase when the power goes off – which still happens just about every day – enjoying a companionable drink and a lively chat in dark surrounds.

CJ, whose partner works a gold mine in a little out-of-the-way place named Teutonic in the Matabeleland South province, competes with me for best bush tale. She also speaks of snakes and scorpions and spiders, of frosts flattening her veggie garden and of pesky wandering goats and dogs. Dogs pinch her braai meat, and vervets pinch my bananas. We text each other, staying in touch when back in the bush, fantasising about some delicious morsel or other and inventing imaginary invitations to meet in an hour or two for cheesecake and cappuccino, which are both in agonisingly short supply unless you live in Harare, on the other side of the country. We share in the ecstasy of our first shower of rain, and commiserate together over our first Kalahari Ferrari of the season. When documentary filming was complete, CJ arrived in town for a pizza and ice-cream celebration that I'd been cruelly tantalising her tastebuds with for months.

Barbara, Dee and I regularly walk the streets in town, to the consternation of the well-to-do whites. It is, apparently, not a particularly conventional thing to do. We play 'spot the white', and will see two or three others over the course of several hours if we're lucky. I'm not sure what they think might happen to them if they did the same, but I've never experienced anything close to harassment.

Well, maybe just once. There's always someone on the streets trying to tempt you with their wares, from bananas to batteries and from pot scourers to pillows. By now I'm used to the recurring '*mukiwa, mukiwa*' ('white person, white person') mantra as you walk by. You get called 'sister', or 'aunty', or 'mama', all labels that you learn to swallow. But when one teenaged boy called me '*gogo*' (pronounced more like ghogho), I nearly tripped over the tree root protruding from the path just ahead of me. *Gogo? Really?* Is that what I looked like now? Like someone's *gogo?* That's downright dreadful! Where on earth did the years go?

I glanced back at him, struggling to conceal my distress, and my mirth. 'You think I'm going to buy anything from you when you call me *granny?*' I shrieked in shocked dismay. *Gogo!* Ouch. That was a leap into a reality I wasn't ready for. Perhaps, I pondered, remarks like these could well be the reason why so few whites dare to walk these streets.

'We're going to the bend-down,' Barbara announced one morning. 'Would you like to join us?'

I knew they were heading for the street market; I just didn't understand the word 'bend-down'.

'Why do you call it the bend-down?' I queried with a frown.

'Because you have to bend down, and rummage through piles of clothing,' Barbara explained with a smile. 'It's a direct translation of *khothama*, the isiNdebele word meaning "to bend down" and that's what the locals call it – the khothama.'

It's another place that white Zimbabweans don't often frequent. It clearly isn't the sort of place to be seen. It is the reason why there are so many well-dressed folk on the streets of Zimbabwe, though. I used to wonder how people, not only in the cities but on the roadsides in the middle of nowhere, could afford to buy such smart clothing. What's more I couldn't find any shops in Bulawayo that sold anything like the items that regularly caught my eye. Then I met Barbara and Dee, who shed light on this puzzling phenomenon.

Bales of clothing arrive from overseas. They're bought by vendors who sell them at both daily and weekend street markets. Most garments are second-hand, although I prefer to think of them as pre-loved, but many are barely worn. I'm astounded by the range of well-known Australian and American labels that mean nothing to the masses. You have to be prepared to spend time, and to dig deep, to find the treasures. Sometimes you're unrewarded, but there are frequently designer labels to be had too from Armani to Calvin Klein, and Columbia Sportswear to Victoria's Secret.

I sit on a bulging pile, in often jam-packed and boisterous surrounds, and sift through it for items that are each going to cost me anything from 25 cents to US$2. I find myself sneering at the vendor, and walking away, when their asking price is an exorbitant US$3 or US$4. I leave contented, having spent a couple of one dollar notes for what, in the First World, would have cost me a couple of hundred. Suitcases full of my clothing were all lost in the January 2011 floods in Australia, so this is the place for me! I figure that the donors of these goods won't mind helping out an unpaid, penny-wise wildlife conservationist.

Barbara walks away in mild disgust when Dee and I hit the piles of soft toys. A *Russ* teddy bear for US$2, a fantastic hippo-cum-novelty pillow for US$3, a floppy elephant, a zebra, a lime green frog (two for a dollar), and many with their tags still on.

'How old are you two?' asks Barbara with a grin.

'After that *gogo* comment, I'm reverting to my second childhood,' I declare.

Dee, who's 19, doesn't bother to respond. She's preoccupied with her search for anything cat-like.

We walk the streets home, a hippo head poking out of my plastic bag, while we search with little success in selected, more upmarket, little stores for blocks of *Nestle* chocolate with smarties in it …

'Tell me again, how old are you?' Barbara jibes.

* * * * *

I'll often walk more than 40 blocks a day carting supplies to take back with me to the bush. When my fresh store of fruit and vegetables – bought from ladies sitting shoulder to shoulder along a designated Bulawayo street – run out, I still, after ten years, live primarily on pasta and tinned fruit. I've progressed a little over the years, though, from locally tinned tomato-and-onion mix to actual pasta sauce imported from South Africa, which has only become available in the last year or two. Pepper grinders can now be found, together with an assortment of tinned cheese sprinkles, although you do need to know where to go to get them. A box of decent South African red is usually available, and so my recurring pasta days are now less likely to make me gag. Zimbabweans finally know what corn chips are, and you can even find salsa on occasion, rather than the make-do tomato-and-onion mix that I once used on everything. With cheese readily available once again, and my splurge on a small microwave after years with only a two-plate hotplate, I can now make myself nachos, although I've never managed to acquire sour cream to dollop on top.

On the odd occasion that I'm in Harare, Carol takes me to a posh supermarket that sometimes has food items imported from America on offer. My best find's been a packet cheesecake, which I now crave, at not too crazy a price. To sachet one, you add butter; to sachet two, you add milk and to sachet three, you add nothing at all, and in just a few minutes you have a really tasty cherry-topped cheesecake on a biscuit base. Now that's my sort of find, but regrettably not available in Bulawayo. Times have certainly changed, though, and these days you can pretty much find whatever you fancy, so long as you're prepared to search around and pay the price.

* * * * *

During the spring months from September to November, in the run-up to the rains, the unusually wide Bulawayo streets are transformed with stunningly beautiful shades of mauve and red. The jacaranda tree is not native to Africa, but its bright-violet canopies are a refreshing, vibrant sight on dusty (and often littered) streets. The poinciana, known as the flamboyant or flame tree, also starts to bloom at this time, and you know that Christmas is close. Its stunning red flowers cluster together to form a glorious umbrella of scarlet. I think back to Christmases in New Zealand and their spectacular pohutukawas, the iconic Kiwi Christmas tree, awash with dazzling crimson flowers. Africa's variety of flame trees are its match. Among the jacarandas and flame trees grow Australian silky oaks, with dark-yellow blooms, adding an extra splash of colour. It's so much more pleasant to wander the streets at this time of year. Don't stand under the silky oaks for too long, though, or you risk being rained on by spittlebugs.

'It's much less dreary in town when all of these beautiful trees are flowering,' I say looking around at the colourful surrounds.

'I hate those jacarandas,' moans Barbara. 'They're messy and they smell.'

I look at her, bewildered. Why is it that city people so often fail to notice the beauty?

'Oh, get a life,' I tell her with a grin.

When the first rains fall in town, after the seven-month dry, people seem to hardly notice. Windows and doors are quickly shut and everyone races inside. When the first rains fall in the bush I've been known to dance around, arms raised skyward, soaked to the skin in joyous thanks, inhaling every last particle of the wonderful earthy smell. In town the first rains smell of wet garbage and greasy roads. I finally understand why there's no celebration here.

Town is a needed change of pace for a few days, and a welcome opportunity to enjoy a drink and a laugh with friends, but there are too many people and far too much noise. Fat from pizza and ice-cream, I am, all too soon, longing to be back in the bush with the elephants.

Garden friends and foes

Myriad different birds are attracted to my six birdbaths in the front yard of my cottage within the grounds of Miombo Safari Camp. The shimmering water also appeals to a particularly friendly, albeit mischievous, vervet monkey troop and two gorgeous bushbuck. There's always a short period of time, several times each day, when everyone seems to arrive at once. I sit on my doorstep and watch a brown-hooded kingfisher share the largest of the birdbaths with a male African paradise-flycatcher, with his stunningly long tail, and a flamboyant red-headed weaver. There are bulbuls and babblers and buntings, together with tinkerbirds, waxbills, thrushes and robins, and a fascinating assortment of other feathered friends all flitting about. Behind them creeps a female bushbuck, soon joined by the playful vervets who have a fondness for tumbling over my outdoor furniture. I love to live among these wild creatures; it's tempting to sit here and simply watch, whiling away the hours.

Late one afternoon I heard a gut-wrenching thud and knew that a bird had flown into one of my windows. I raced outside, horrified to see a small clump of deep-blue feathers lying still, on the ground. As I moved closer I realised that it was an exquisite African pygmy kingfisher, and it was alive. I gently cupped the tiny creature in the palm of my hands, where he fitted easily, and sat with him on my garden bench, allowing him time to recover. He stayed on my knee for a good ten minutes, gradually becoming more and more animated. As I studied his superb, shiny colouring I worried that he may have broken something, but to my relief he bobbed his tiny head one last time and whizzed off like an overgrown grasshopper.

A few days later I looked up to discover a snake in one of the

Zambezi teak trees that's only a few metres from my front door, and my heart jumped into my mouth. Snakes, I don't need. At first I convinced myself that it must be a harmless spotted bush snake. But then I grabbed binoculars, and felt a hot flush course through my body. 'Perhaps this is what menopause is going to feel like!' I thought. It definitely wasn't a spotted bush snake. It was very slender and much too long for my liking. The top of its head was green and there was an orange band running through its eye. The body was grey with diagonal bands flecked with black and orange. It was a vine snake. 'Oh, please, not a vine snake,' I mumbled.

My reference books provided additional information that I really didn't need to know.

It's not commonly seen.

'Then why am I so privileged?' I muttered to myself with a frown.

It lays up to 13 eggs during November/December.

'Lovely! It'll be November in just two weeks time.'

Its venom is almost as potent as that of a boomslang.

'A *boomslang*? Oh man, give me a break.'

It will sit unmoving for hours, waiting for its prey.

Feeling anxious, but morbidly fascinated, I observed it, on and off, for hours, and it didn't move. It just lay there, head protruding, body curled up inside what I had previously thought was a great little bushbaby sleeping house: a small hollow log that someone had secured to the branches of this tree years ago. I grabbed the 'snake blocker' that Craig and Amos had made for me, and plonked it against my open front door with a thud. I hadn't been terribly vigilant about making use of these screens, but that would now change I decided. Suddenly, though, they seemed utterly inadequate. I reckoned I could do with something that covered my entire house!

I glanced over at my 4x4, parked just a few metres away, on the opposite side of my front door. Except when it was raining, it always stood with no roof-cover. I'd parked it under a leafy tree, for protection from the searing sun. I had a rule about not parking directly under the branches of trees, whenever I was inside it, ever since the day in the field when a horribly long green snake (probably a boomslang) had landed on the bonnet of my 4x4. A metre further back and it would have come through my open roof and landed right on top of me. I relaxed my rule, though, whenever I wasn't sitting inside it. Not anymore. I didn't fancy climbing in to start my vehicle, only to have to deal with a deadly snake slithering out from under a seat.

I was really starting to get the creeps. Only two nights before, I was in the shower and spotted the largest baboon spider I'd ever seen, on the shower curtain. After an appalled gasp, so deep and sudden that it left me feeling faint, he was quickly – horrifically – dispatched. Then there was a speedy little scorpion-like creature, which dashed around at rapid speed. The next night I had frogs. I actually really like frogs, but how so many little, stripy fellows, with bulging eyes, had managed to get into my bathroom I couldn't quite figure out. The first showers of the season had fallen, always such an exhilarating time, but it did come with a downside. The critters were resurfacing. It seemed like it had actually rained frogs! This puzzled me since there was nowhere close by where tadpoles could have hatched. I hadn't realised that the bushveld rain frog lays its eggs in trees, rather than in water, which hatch into froglets rather than tadpoles. These little fellows completely bypass the tadpole stage. I'd become mother to a whole swag of tiny frogs, each about four centimetres long.

The snake sighting wasn't doing my blood pressure any good at all, even though it had probably only come to eat the frogs, so I eventually decided to leave him be and resume my daily dose of computer work. Fifteen minutes later, still feeling decidedly distracted, I was once again standing at my front door, binoculars in hand. I searched first with my naked eye, and then raised the binoculars to my face. The vine snake was gone. I stepped over the short screen, and edged a few paces closer to the tree. The snake was definitely gone. This was even worse. 'Gone *where*?' I shuddered.

* * * * *

CJ, Barbara and I decided one evening, while we were sitting together on those Bulawayo stairs enjoying a few tots, that when one of us was feeling particularly fed up we'd text each other this rather strange phrase: 'There's a cow in my kitchen!' Or, when something was exceptionally exasperating: 'There's a fuckin' cow in my kitchen!' The first time I did this after my return to Hwange, CJ replied, 'Is there really?' This made me laugh. CJ knows that in my bush life *anything* is possible. She must have had a tot too many that evening, and had momentarily forgotten our little joke.

Incidentally (and much to my dismay), a herd of cows has actually wandered past my cottage. Now, I looked up from my laptop and gasped. I grabbed my mobile phone. 'There's a fuckin' *donkey* in my kitchen!' I texted. It wasn't quite in my kitchen, but it was right there, just outside my door, its head over my snake screen. I don't think anybody believed me; they just thought I was taking liberties with the word 'cow'.

It was my second attempt at planting grass runners, after torturous days, and then weeks, of no water. 'Don't you even think about it,' I moaned, glaring at this odd, white creature and waving my arms in the air. I imagined those hind legs delivering an impressive kick. The donkey just stood there, being a typical ass. It looked too much like a sad old horse. And everybody knows by now how I feel about horses.

Willa

One of the illustrious members of Whole's family who deserves a special mention is the adult female named Willa. With the moist fingers of her trunk frequently hovering high above my head, Willa never fails to remind me of one of those huge, gushy, slobbering dogs. Although she can certainly be mischievous, Willa, with a distinctive square notch that juts from the middle of her left ear, is an affable soul. Our relationship has deepened over the years to one of mutual trust and sheer delight in each other's company.

A few years passed before Willa revealed her true personality to me. Whole was always the shining star in this sub-family, and Willa tended to linger happily in the background. When I first met her, she was a quiet and rather bashful elephant. The extended W family was the first group of elephants that I mapped a family tree for, and so I spent a great deal of time with them in my early years, observing and documenting their relationships with one another. I came to know them well. By 2003 Willa was slowly becoming more inquisitive and was joining Whole for prolonged visits around my 4x4. It wasn't until 2004 that our relationship grew deeper.

It was the time of land take-overs on the Hwange Estate and everyone, including the elephants and me, was uneasy. Few others were saying it out loud but gunfire was out of control at this time. The elephants were moving in large aggregations, probably for safety's sake. On this particular morning, even I heard the spine-chilling shots. No infrasonic ability was needed. One minute there were no elephants in sight and the next scores of them were racing, terrified, out from the tree line. There were several families fleeing in tight formation, with ears flat and tails out. One of them was Whole's.

It took me hours to find the W family again after that distressing episode, and another two hours to regain just a little of their confidence. It was Willa who came close to my vehicle before the others in her family. She approached hesitantly, while I alternated between singing 'Amazing Grace' and talking gently to her, reassuring her that everything was alright, despite knowing that it clearly wasn't. Just as most family members were beginning to settle, a game-drive vehicle approached and the elephants took off into the bush yet again at speed, in complete silence. Now they were frightened of a game-drive vehicle, but curiously always of that specific game-drive vehicle. I was increasingly suspicious of so many things that were going on at this time – things that were scaring the life out of these elephants.

When I finally found the W family again the next day, I spent the entire morning with them. I didn't know the word to describe it back then, but I know now that this was *masakhe*. I was already attempting to rebuild that which had been broken.

Willa stayed close by my 4x4 that day, leaving only to drink. Since then, we've enjoyed a special friendship. From my 'baby names' booklet, which helps me to select names for the elephants, I knew that Willa was a diminutive of Wilhelmina, which means 'the protectress'. I protect her, and she protects me. We protect each other.

When I began coaching some of the photographic-safari guides about the Presidential Elephants, Willa was one of those they received an extra-special introduction to. She always seemed to want to climb *inside* my 4x4 with me. She was also a flirt, I realised, and quickly became familiar with the male guides.

Whenever I call to the W family, sometimes from a hundred or more metres away, Willa frequently leads the accelerated procession towards me. Cynthia Moss, of Amboseli elephant fame, calls it 'the floppy run'. It's a loose way of running, where their head, ears and trunk wave about, in pure pachyderm pleasure, as they stride forward. That wild animals should come when they're called is something special, but when they come with such enthusiasm it's something truly extraordinary.

It was while the documentary film crew were with me in September

2011, that my relationship with Willa reached a new level of intensity. For me, it was a profoundly powerful moment in time, captured on film.

I don't often see adult Presidential Elephants lying down. It's just not what they tend to do, unless they're unwell, although I'm aware that other elephant populations are observed asleep on their side quite frequently. I was concerned when Willa unexpectedly lay down beside the mineral licks at Mpofu pan, under a blazing sun. I hadn't recorded when she was last in oestrus but thought, based on the age of her youngest calf, and her own inter-birth intervals, that it would be at least another four months before she had another baby. So if she wasn't soon to give birth, perhaps she was sick? The days were hot. Perhaps she was simply exhausted.

Once she got back on her feet it was only a few minutes before she wandered over to the shade of a teak tree, and lay down on her side once more. I waited for her to rise, and then drove towards her, stopping just a few metres away. 'Hey Willa girl. Are you alright my Willa?' I still didn't know whether or not there was something wrong with her, although the cameramen did pick up something pulsating in the side of her huge, grey body.

Willa wandered towards me, and stopped just centimetres away, as she always does. I talked to her, as I always do. And then something exceptional happened. Willa rested her trunk on the ground, and put what felt like her full weight against the driver-side door. I felt my 4x4 shift, and understood that she could toss it on its side like a matchstick, with me inside. But I knew this wasn't her intention. She wanted company. She wanted comfort. She wanted me to reassure her that everything would be alright. While tenderly touching her trunk with the back of my hand, I put my face against the long leathery nose of this wild giant and kissed her gently. This was not a hurried encounter. This was two beings, totally at peace with one another.

I looked up over the rim of my glasses, into Willa's eyes, and held her gaze. I kissed her again, and again. Willa stayed just as she was, looking down on me with kind, wise eyes. What was she thinking? This enormous, several-ton, wild animal who was choosing to commune so very closely with a human being. I say to the sceptics, 'There's no need to spend your time trying to convince me that she wasn't thinking and trying to communicate in her own way.' This intelligent being, gifted with conscious thoughts and emotions, was most definitely thinking. She may not be able to speak our language, nor we hers, but this does not mean that she has no level of understanding or that she's incapable of comprehending. On some level she understands me. After more than a decade of living among these giants and learning to know them intimately, something that few in this world have ever had the privilege to do, no one will ever convince me otherwise. And this, I recalled forlornly, is an animal that the human species likes to hunt and kill.

There's no doubt that wild elephants enjoy the social stimulation of being with their own kind. I'm certain that they also enjoy the social stimulation of being with a human being who they trust.

This encounter with Willa left me feeling euphoric. To have gained such trust from an enormous wild animal, and one that has been through many troubled times, makes everything worthwhile. No human could thank you so well.

When I shared the photo of me kissing Willa, the one that adorns the back cover of this book, with my hippo-friend Karen, she wept. She wept because she understands it all, because to people like her it isn't just a photo. It's a whole, telling, story in itself.

Christmastide

The song, 'The Twelve Days of Christmas' is a Yuletide classic. The verses that I learnt in childhood describe a gift given on each of these 12 festive days, beginning on Christmas Day and running through to the 5th of January. With wine in hand a few years ago, in preparation for our much yearned-for Christmas break, which we were spending with our friend Dinks, Shaynie and I decided that these lyrics needed to be varied to reflect a proper Hwange Christmas. There were, after all, no partridges in pear trees here. So, we sipped chilled wine and chuckled, and in a remarkably short space of time came up with our own exclusive Hwange version, which we now recall every festive season:

On the first day of Christmas,
My true love sent to me
An elephant in a mud bath.

On the second day of Christmas,
My true love sent to me
Two crimson shrikes, and
An elephant in a mud bath.

And so it went on, until:

On the twelfth day of Christmas,
My true love sent to me
Twelve shots of Amarula,
Eleven spiders biting,

Ten warthogs wallowing,
Nine kudus leaping,
Eight shrews a chewing,
Seven buffaloes bellowing,
Six savannah sunsets,
F---i---v---e rhi---nos charging,
Four lions snoring,
Three friends a singing,
Two crimson shrikes, and
An elephant in a mud bath.

We were quite chuffed with ourselves and promptly went about printing and laminating our masterpiece.

There's not much frenzy in the prelude to a Zimbabwean bush Christmas. Festive preparations are minimal compared to the First World flurry although Shaynie did splurge on a (rather scarce) turkey and we searched the Bulawayo streets, successfully in the end, for (even more elusive) cranberry sauce. It was agreed that we'd dress formally and, with white tablecloth, champagne and candles, we would eat under the stars in the stunning Matobo Hills, about 30 kilometres south of Bulawayo. Of course it rained. So we set up inside our rustic accommodation instead, looking out over the splendidly sculptured granite boulders and wooded valleys of this timeless place, breathing in the grandeur and the mystique of the Maleme Gorge, pretending to be classier than we really are. It was the first and only time I've seen Shaynie in a dress, and it was a long one at that. She even clomped around in high heels, which, come to think of it, probably brought on the ill-timed rain.

Our Christmas decorations consisted in part of seeds and pods and feathers and wildflowers, which are so much more pleasing than the commercial alternatives. There were no reindeers but there was a horse, a few of them in fact. Horse riding is actually on offer around Maleme Dam, but the horses are really cheeky. After one gave me a hell of a fright by poking its head, and its whooping teeth, through the window of our vehicle, I was keeping my distance. Dinks and Shaynie approached them nonchalantly. Then, all of a sudden, 'Arrrrhhhhhhhh!' That squeal came from Dinks, and if looks could kill that horse would be dead by now. It appeared as if the horse had Dinks by the neck. No wait, by the ear … what on earth was going on?

I have to admit that by this time I was laughing hysterically, but with deep concern, I swear. Dinks' sparkling blue earrings had caught the mischievous horse's attention. He'd stolen one out of her ear. Thankfully, he hadn't swallowed it and Dinks, with a sigh of relief and bewilderment, recovered it from the ground. The horse had given her quite a nip.

'And you wonder why I'm nervous around horses,' I bleated. It seemed to me that, like with the elephants, everyone should stay inside their vehicle, which is where we all scrambled to.

It's always a bit scary going to Matobo with Shaynie. She forever wants to climb something. 'I'm heading up that *gomo*,' she announces, with her sights set on some horribly high rocky outcrop. I followed her only once. The walk was long and agonising. I could barely breathe. Wheezing uncontrollably, I collapsed at the top, swearing never to do it again.

'Look at this view,' Shaynie crooned.

'I like the view perfectly well from the bottom thanks,' I declared.

The Matobo Hills is the sort of place that makes you want to pack a gourmet picnic lunch, not just at Christmas, but at any time of the year, and bask in the scenic surrounds, from the perfectly picturesque *bottom* of a *gomo*. Now with delicious food items more readily available in a few Bulawayo shops, I tempt Shaynie, who is tired of the repetitious staff food she's fed in the Hwange bush, with a simple, but rapturous, menu:

Crispy bread rubbed with slow-roasted tomatoes
Baked red peppers bathed in olive oil and sprinkled with basil
Smoked mussels with finely chopped bacon, topped with olive pesto
Mushrooms sautéed in butter, garlic and parsley

Multi-coloured lettuce, slick with olive oil and sprinkled with feta cheese and freshly ground black pepper

Pink champagne and slabs of gouda cheese and fat, purple grapes

Cashew nut and coconut chocolate

I'm not a vegetarian, but I always enjoy it more when what I eat has no resemblance to a living creature. I was suffering from indigestion just thinking about this feast; a rare day with no pasta or tinned fruit or tinned vegetable curry. I kissed the tips of my fingers in anticipation. '*Magnifique!*' we agreed.

One day soon we'd do it, we pledged. Maybe this Christmas.

A *spirit messenger*

Things sometimes happen to me in the Hwange bush that I just can't explain. And perhaps, as the saying goes, some things are true whether we believe in them or not.

Since Andy's sudden death in March of 2000, strange things – some would say coincidental things – keep occurring. But I'm no longer sure that I believe in coincidence.

I remember the days following Andy's death as if they happened only yesterday: the upset, the disbelief, the anxiety and his funeral in the Hwange bush, which I flew from Australia to attend. Andy believed that my true calling was in the African bush and his emails constantly encouraged me to take the leap into the unknown, but I hadn't done so yet. He was my inspiration, my hero.

I can still see the extraordinary shaft of bright light that fell to earth the day after he was laid to rest; it was a mysterious, and instant, response to my call for 'a sign' from him. In the presence of others I dismissed it as coincidence, but I was never really convinced. The photograph of this astonishing ray of light, unlike the thousands of other photos in my doomed storeroom in flood-ravaged Queensland, was with me in Zimbabwe when the inland tsunami hit, and therefore survived. Of all of the photographs that I've ever taken, this one haunts me the most.

A few days after Andy's funeral I spent the day at Umtshibi – where he, Lol and their young son Drew had lived – helping Lol as she began the arduous task of dealing with Andy's things. It was dark by now and, although I had special permission to exit the national park at any time by an alternate route, since the tourist gate closed at sunset, it was time for me to leave. Just before I headed off, Lol read me a poem with heart-rending words about living on and doing all things the same. Tears filled my eyes. She encouraged me, even though it should have been the other way around, to keep enjoying the park as I had when Andy was alive. We said our goodbyes and I drove away sadly, knowing that I'd probably never return to this National Parks' house.

Then something else happened that I've never forgotten. At the Umtshibi turnoff I turned right towards Main Camp. Only metres up the road I suddenly found myself behind the enormous backside of a lone bull elephant. He appeared from nowhere and began walking right in the middle of the road, his trunk swaying from side to side and dragging along the ground. I switched off my headlights and waited, hoping that he'd move out of my way. He didn't. I followed him, and followed him, travelling at his chosen speed of less than ten kilometres per hour. I stopped frequently, and switched off my headlights. It made no difference. He had no intention of moving aside.

I'd never before known an elephant to continue to walk in the middle of the road for such a long period of time. All of a sudden I felt nervous. I was alone in the African bush. It was dark. I reached around and locked all of my car doors. Then I laughed at myself, wondering if I really believed that some wild African animal was actually going to try to open my doors! The uneasy feeling evaporated and I looked towards the sky and smiled. 'Okay Andy,' I said light-heartedly without deliberation, 'you've had your fun!' This was such typical Andy Searle humour and I could feel him grinning down on me.

I hoped that Lol wouldn't be worried. She'd asked me to phone her when I was back at my lodgings, so that she knew I'd arrived safely. I was already at least 15 minutes delayed. 'Come on Andy, I've had enough now!' I heard myself say out loud. But nothing changed. My huge uninvited fellow traveller was still right where he wanted to be. More time passed and then finally – *finally* – he moved off to my right. I smiled and light-heartedly asked Andy what he had in store for me now.

Incredibly, a gregarious, bucking wildebeest appeared instantly to my left, startling me. It raced along the roadside, right beside my vehicle. I went through the process again, stopping temporarily and switching off my headlights. 'Oh come on Andy,' I jested, 'give me a break!' It was hilarious. For almost a minute I had a crazy, bucking wildebeest as a companion. He eventually moved off too and the drive became quiet and peaceful.

When I finally arrived at my lodge I rang Lol. I told her about the elephant and the wildebeest that had delayed me, not saying anything about my words to Andy. 'It was a gift from Andrew,' Lol said to me. Twelve years later I still wonder if it actually was.

Soon after I arrived to live in the Hwange bush, one year after Andy's death, I began having unusually frequent encounters with bateleurs that I couldn't explain. The bateleur is a stunning bird, although its one that I hadn't paid any particular attention to. It's a large black eagle, adorned with bright red on the face and legs, that glides effortlessly through the sky with wing tips pointing upwards.

As I became increasingly involved in heart-rending activities like snare removals and battles for the elephants' land, I'd constantly see bateleurs at my most vulnerable times. I found them strangely comforting. It was in 2004 that I first announced flippantly to a friend, 'I think Andy's come back as a bateleur.'

It was months later that I learnt that some of the Shona people of Zimbabwe believe the bateleur to be a spirit messenger, and I felt no hint of surprise. They are said to bring protection and good fortune.

Still today, I think of Andy every time I see a bateleur and continue to marvel at the uncanny timing when one will unexpectedly appear and linger for unusually lengthy periods of time. On the day that I returned to Hwange in 2011 after being evicted from my home, more uncertain than ever about what lay ahead, a bateleur flew with me for several kilometres as I turned off the Victoria Falls–Bulawayo road, heading towards Hwange National Park Main Camp.

Although always inexplicably calmed, the cynic in me reverts to the theory of coincidence. More and more often, though, I recall the movie *City of Angels*, and that haunting line, 'Some things are true whether you believe in them or not.'

Over the railway line

When I think of the railway line that runs through Dete, which stretches all of the way from the Cape to Cairo, a poignant image materialises before my eyes. It's a photograph that was taken of Andy not long before he died: a heart-rending vision of father and young son, with the railway line disappearing into the distance. It's a haunting shot (my copy destroyed in the Queensland floods but the image lingers, etched in my mind) that gives the impression of time vanishing, as if Andy knew that he'd soon be on a journey to somewhere else.

I'd never before been so aware of the railway line until I moved into my new home at Miombo. The train drivers seem to believe that if they have to be awake at 3 a.m. then everyone else should be too. Their needless, prolonged hooting, night after night, certainly took some getting used to; in truth, I'm still not used to it yet.

The railway line is a key Hwange landmark. The Presidential and other elephants know it well. It's what separates the Hwange Estate from Hwange National Park. There are no fences, or other physical boundaries. The elephants wander across, on their way from one waterhole to the next. Some, tragically, lose their lives in the crossing.

I venture over the railway line only occasionally. It feels a little like I'm going on holiday when I do so, even though it's just down the road. For me the national park has a feel not at all like the estate, and this isn't just because I'm generally not working when I travel there. It's a revitalising change of pace and scenery; the whole ambience of the place is pleasantly different from what I'm used to.

Unlike the estate where there's (sometimes) the steady flow of municipal water and quieter electric pumps operating, Hwange

National Park is abuzz with the sound of diesel engines thrusting life-giving water into pans. There are stunning, wide open spaces, and impressive numbers of elephants and long-limbed giraffes ambling past iconic African trees. There's a comforting sense of freedom and space as you drive around at your own pace.

It wasn't a particularly uplifting experience, however, when I crossed the railway line during the lead-up to the November 2011 full moon. It was nearly mid-month and no rain of note had fallen. Full moon hadn't brought with it any change in the weather. It was hot, and it was dry. Temperatures hovered in the mid to high 40s (over 115 degrees Fahrenheit). There wasn't a cloud in the sky. There was the smell of death and despair around the pans. The water situation was desperate, despite various concerned groups making a concerted effort to keep the diesel pumps running.

Elephants, both big and little, were dead, and some carcasses were clearly visible from the roadsides. There was still plenty of grass and other vegetation for the wildlife to eat, except around the tourists' favourite Nyamandlovu platform, which looked desert-like. The elephants had to be dying from insufficient drinking water; the smaller ones were weakened and succumbing more readily to hungry lions.

I sat and watched the elephants' reaction to the bloated carcass of an adult female who'd died right beside Nyamandlovu pan less than 36 hours before, her fallen hide stained white with the faeces of vultures. Her tusks had not yet been removed. I'd never seen elephants react with such disinterest to the death of one of their own. In the two hours that I watched, scores of elephant families – if you could call them families – came and went. After a quick count of adults relative to youngsters, combined with a rough age census, I knew immediately when a family wasn't intact. There were adult females obviously missing from many of the groups. Some elephants were travelling with just two or three members, which is something that you don't ever see among the Presidential Elephants except in times of severe disturbance. Not even one elephant stopped to pay their respects or investigate the deceased female. This, too, was such contrary behaviour to that of the elephants I know so well. I was saddened and disturbed by what I saw.

Whether this was an already-fragmented population (Were adult female elephants being poached or ration-hunted?), or whether the missing females had recently succumb to insufficient water, I could not know from my limited observation time. Whether or not the lack of interest in the dead elephant was a result of some deeper cause, or if it was on account of the elephants' stress levels at this point in time, I couldn't know either. But things didn't feel right. There was certainly inadequate water in every pumped pan that I visited, and this had to be contributing to the weakened state of the elephants, and therefore to the numerous deaths, but it seemed like there were more questions begging answers. I left wishing that I could just sit and enjoy watching elephants again, without always analysing what I saw.

A vehicle pulled up beside mine just down the road from Nyamandlovu platform. I lifted my eyes from my note pad and glanced around.

'Do you remember John?' asked the man behind the steering wheel.

My eyes shifted to the vehicle's back seat where a grinning man was seated. It certainly wasn't John Foster. Then a smile split my face. Of course I remembered who this John was. It was 13 years ago, in Christmas of 1998, that we found ourselves volunteering our time on the same bird-ringing project at Ngulia Safari Lodge in the Tsavo West National Park in Kenya.

John muttered our principal investigator's name with a roll of his eyes.

'How on earth do you remember his name?' I exclaimed, immediately realising that I still knew it too. He had, after all, almost wiped us all out on our very first day in Kenya when we came dangerously close to plunging over a steep roadwork embankment while he was driving us to Tsavo. Squashed together in the back of his vehicle, which was hurtling along at ridiculous speed, the small team of volunteers was immediately bonded. By fear.

For 12 days we were awoken at crazy hours to extract birds from nets. The words, 'This cannot be healthy' were muttered on many occasions when, after crawling out of bed, we were frequently overwhelmed by laughter – brought on primarily, I think, from lack of sleep.

Mist regularly engulfs Ngulia Safari Lodge at Christmas time and this mist, together with the lights of the lodge, confuses migrating birds, attracting them to the nets below. It's considered one of the bird wonders of the world. We all just wondered what the heck we were doing there.

In truth we had a fantastic time and it was certainly a memorable Christmas. We celebrated with an African Santa Claus, and crazy numbers of hurtling dung beetles that were also attracted to the lights of the lodge.

Almost 8,000 birds were studied and ringed during our time in Tsavo, the results used to guide and justify the importance of a chain of wetland reserves to provide safe passage for migratory birds. Unlike some volunteer projects, where you don't feel that you've contributed anything real, we all went home exhausted and satisfied.

John now lives in neighbouring Botswana. He said he'd read my books.

'Right now I'm looking for something positive to write about,' I declared gazing around me with a frown.

'I think you're in the wrong country for that,' John smiled.

It was like old times, the laughter flowing freely. Those 13 years had gone by in a flash. I told him about the documentary that would soon be screening.

'You'll be famous,' he declared.

'Or is that infamous?' I queried with a smile.

'You're already that,' he smirked.

I drove around some more, revelling in the vibrant flush of new, spring leaf that had appeared in anticipation of the rains. Abdim's and woolly-necked storks had arrived with the same expectation. It's always good to see them. In the distance, thick bushfire smoke billowed skyward. It was scorching hot. We desperately needed rain.

Eventually I returned to Nyamandlovu pan where I noticed, now that I wasn't so preoccupied with the elephants, that the hippos were having an equally difficult time. They were caked in thick, grey mud. Peering at them through binoculars, to where they were slumped in the middle of the almost-dry pan, I wondered bleakly if they were dead. Then I detected the twitching of an ear and knew they were just doing what they could to shield themselves from the blistering rays of the sun. Among the feasting marabou storks and hundreds of vultures there was a solitary snow-white egret, looking acutely out of place in this dell of despair.

I parked for a while in the shade of the tall platform for a little respite of my own from the blazing sun. A troop of baboons were seeking shelter too, scampering about above me on the platform's wooden floor. All of a sudden there was a splattering of liquid on my note pad, splashing all over my body. I looked up through my open roof, and through the cracks of the floorboards above me, and cursed. It was not exactly the shower I was longing for. I was being peed on, with perfect precision, by a baboon.

Sections of some of the roads were awfully corrugated, and in places terribly potholed. I was always grateful to arrive at the next pan in one piece. I came upon the less-frequently seen sable and roan antelopes, and lions too, but around every fast-drying pan things were rather dreary and depressing. I decided that I'd cross over the railway line again in December, after rain had fallen, to witness the much longed-for metamorphosis from barren to abundance.

*****

By late December there'd been some rain but not nearly as much as was needed to properly fill the pans. Some on the estate still only held meagre amounts of water. I'd planned to return to the national park on Christmas Eve, but although everything looked leafy and green it barely even felt like the wet season. I decided to put my day trip off a little longer.

It turned out to be a memorable Christmas nonetheless. Just as the clock ticked past midnight, ushering in Christmas Eve 2011, I parted my mosquito net and slipped into bed. Sitting up, I pegged the net closed using a clothes peg, as I'd learnt was a sensible thing to do, and reached towards the wall beside me to switch off my bedroom light.

'What on earth is *that*?' I muttered, squinting through the netting towards a substantial black splodge on the wall in front of me. 'You have to be kidding me …'

I hesitantly parted the mosquito net once more and crept out of bed to grab my glasses. I almost wish I hadn't put them on. There on my white wall was the most enormous black scorpion that I'd ever seen. It looked like there was a black *lobster* on my wall. Its tail curved backwards over its body. Its pincers were wide, thick and huge. It looked not unlike an armoured tank.

'What the … What on earth is this thing doing on my *wall?*' I lamented to myself with an uncontrollable shiver. 'Aren't scorpions meant to live under rocks or something? Look how unbelievably *big* this sucker is.' It had to be more than 15 centimetres long. 'Okay, okay, I can do this.' I crept closer in sheer disbelief. It definitely looked like something you'd eat in a seafood restaurant, or perhaps something that might eat you.

I'd been battling with Kalahari Ferraris inside my cottage since the first rain had fallen. I'd never seen so many of these rapid-running scary creatures in my life. But they were nothing compared to this. I recalled people saying to always check inside your shoes for scorpions. This one would barely even fit in a shoe.

I'd never get to sleep again if I allowed this creature to stay where it was, even though I knew that given its size it probably wasn't overly venomous. One might die of fright just looking at it, though. There was no way that I could attempt to capture it alive and relocate it. It was just too scary. It was midnight, I couldn't call on anybody. It simply had to go.

Armed with a sturdy flip-flop and *Baygon*, and with a wildly palpitating heart (and, I confess, an occasional scream), I managed to dispatch the giant arachnid. I felt awful having done so and spent hours trying to get to sleep.

The next morning I took photographs – it was somewhat less horrifying and smaller-looking now that it was deceased – and emailed them to Carol. I didn't have any scorpion reference books or satisfactory internet facility to be able to ID this critter myself.

The data and photos that Carol emailed back matched my exhibit exactly. Some were telling me that it was probably a rock scorpion, since they're common in southern Africa, but it looked precisely like an emperor scorpion to us – the largest of the scorpion species, and not often included in southern African reference books.

'Dozens can live together in colonies,' her clippings read.

Dozens? In colonies? Holy crap ...

'Eats mostly termites. And crickets.'

I'd just had an invasion of termites, munching my front door from the inside out and emerging through cracks in my floor. Only the day before I'd painstakingly taken my door off its hinges and poured *Doom: Blue Death* into its innards. I awoke to monster crickets on my shower curtain most mornings.

'Can be found under rocks, logs and other forest debris.'

And, evidently, on people's *walls*!

'*On the first day of Christmas my true love gave to me, a scorp-i-on on my bedroom wall ...*'

Clearly, Shaynie and I had got the words wrong when we rewrote this song.

'*On the second day of Christmas my true love gave to me, two Kalahari Ferraris and a scorp-i-on on my bedroom wall ...*'

'*On the third day of Christmas my true love gave to me, three baboon spiders, two Kalahari Ferraris and a scorp-i-on on my bedroom wall ...*'

A girlfriend, contemplating another festive season family gathering, emailed to say that she'd happily trade my scorpion for her relatives. Then she saw my photograph. 'Okay. You can keep it,' she wrote. 'You win.'

* * * * *

Rain was still scarce, with not a cloud in the sky early in the new year, and I decided it was time to journey back into Hwange National Park regardless. Amid delightful waves of light-lemon-coloured butterflies known as African migrants fluttering all around me, I drove towards the railway line.

What I noticed first of all was that the round, red lights on the railway crossing markers were no longer flashing. It seemed to me that they'd been blinking, or more often on solid, for the most part of the past decade, certainly whenever I ventured this way. I didn't trust them at all and slowed anyway, to make certain that a train wasn't about to flatten me, before crossing over.

Stunning flame lilies were visible along the roadsides. The area around Nyamandlovu platform, that had previously looked so barren, was covered in a carpet of green dotted with tiny, blue flowers. Masses of yellow-billed kites circled in the cloudless sky, and striking carmine bee-eaters, with their distinctive deep chirp, flitted about among hundreds of brightly coloured dragonflies. The white, foam nests of tree frogs hung from fallen logs and gorgeous crowned cranes wandered about. White-faced ducks whistled their enchanting call as I soaked up the splendour of the green season, amused by the playful antics of eight delightful warthog piglets and a crèche of baby impalas. The pan was now full but there was little other surface water about. Everything looked lush and promising, but much more rain was needed.

The elephant carcass in front of the platform had been removed. The herds of elephants had all gone elsewhere, probably deep into the bush as they always do at this time of year. During my day in the park I didn't see an elephant, not even a lone bull. The hippos were no longer forced to live in mud. They honked their contentment in their watery home.

What I always get most pleasure from while in Hwange National Park are the giraffes. Scores of these stately creatures amble about in groups, elegant and grand, looking as if they haven't got a care in the world. I watch their fluid movements, envying their peaceful existence. If I wasn't so engrossed with elephants, I'd spend more time with giraffes. I imagine they have a deeper story of their own, just waiting to be told.

Late in the afternoon, after a pleasurable day inside the park, I crossed back over the railway line into more familiar territory. None of the estate pans were full of water as yet. We'd clearly had even less rain on this side of the railway line and I longed for soaking downpours.

I drove the estate roads home, wondering what the new year might have in store for me. There would be more battles, for sure. I had learnt by now that this is Zimbabwe's way.

The veld was quiet. Just like the jumbos inside the park, sightings of the Presidential Elephant families are always relatively few at this time of year.

I missed them all. I wished them well. I yearned for them to stay safe.

Afterword

2011 turned out to be my most satisfying year in Africa to date. Against the odds, I rebuilt my Hwange life once more – much to the chagrin of some, which made it an even sweeter triumph. The reaffirmation of the Presidential decree was a coup that I'll always take pride in. There was the exhausting filming for the international television documentary, where the Presidential Elephants validated themselves as being among the most extraordinary wild animals in the world. Then there was the writing of this book, which is another attempt to raise vital awareness. And all of this following the devastating Australian floods where I lost most of what I once had to fall back on.

All of this toil and extra time and energy spent trying to slay those dreaded dragons, and yet the aggravations continue on much the same as before, with no end in sight. I sometimes feel like I'm trapped in my own *Groundhog Day*. Year after year after year, nothing really changes, except the *nature* of the hassles.

I frequently feel that I'm becoming too tired of it all – particularly when my roof is leaking in a downpour, or routinely releasing thatch dirt over everything, or termites have emerged through cracks in the floor to demolish my grass mats, or there's once again no fuel in Dete, or no electricity, or perhaps no water for days on end. But then I open a bottle of bubbles and chase that fuckin' cow *out* of my kitchen …

The thing about change is that, in the end, it nearly always turns out for the best. Despite the non-stop frustrations of living as I do, I really enjoy the secluded spot near Miombo Safari Camp where I live, with its bushy surrounds, stunning birdlife and all manner of wildlife wandering through. My cherished friendships with the elephants continue to go from strength to strength. New human friendships have been forged and old ones revived.

I've been quick, though, to distance myself from things that don't sit right with me. There are, sadly, some who have over-promoted themselves, making out that they know more about the Presidential Elephants than they really do, and pretending to do far more for them than they actually do. These are groups that typically don't see it as advantageous for their guides – many of whom know a mere handful of elephants and very little else about them – to be properly trained. Instead, they see dollar signs, enticing the tourists in based on the Presidential Elephants, even if it means misleadingly inflating their offerings and their contribution to conservation. Sometimes this has been with the misuse of my name, making promises that they already know I cannot honour, but they make them anyway. I can only suggest to prospective tourists that you do your homework and support only those Hwange Estate lodges that have the elephants' interests, and not merely their own, at heart. Support those who plough some of your tourist dollars directly back into their welfare. Support those lodges that proactively provide dry season water for them, in areas where they game-drive and not just at their own lodge waterhole. Support those who bother to learn something real about them, and who keep up-to-date with their lives. The elephants will be grateful.

I return often, in my mind at least, to that Sunshine Coast beach in Queensland and ask myself, over and over again, that million dollar question: 'Is Zimbabwe where I want to continue to spend my dash?' I still have no idea. These days I take it just one day at a time, without certainty or security, constantly battling those absurd dragons but nonetheless convinced now that one person can indeed make a difference. You just have to dig your heels in, and go for it.

Acknowledgements

I am particularly indebted to long-standing friends who have continually supported and encouraged me through difficult times – Dinks Adlam, Shaynie Beswick, Bobby Dempsey, Eileen Duffy, John Foster, Mandy Keating, Carol McCammon, Andrea McKain, Henry Nel, Karen Paolillo and Lol Searle.

To Miombo Safari Camp, the Ministry of the Environment and Natural Resources, Dawn Properties, the Forestry Commission, Ganda Lodge and the Parks & Wildlife Management Authority for gracious support in tough times.

To Esther van der Meer and her husband Hans Dullemont for invaluable snare-removal assistance.

To Craig Haskins, Laurie Simpson, Bev Staak, Barbara Strydom and CJ van den Berg for laughter and help when it's been needed most.

A special thank you to Mandy Keating who created, and generously maintains, sharonpincott.com; to Bobby Dempsey for taking the time to review my manuscript as I wrote and for proffering valuable feedback; to Andrea McKain who kindly completed a final run-through of my manuscript. And to Shaynie Beswick for my home away from home in Bulawayo, from where I get numerous town tasks done.

I'm grateful to the scores of people who wrote to tell me that my last book touched their lives, and who encouraged me to keep at it, and to continue to write.

To Bridget Impey, Kerrie Barlow, Amy Flatau and the rest of the team at Jacana Media for their enthusiasm, and to Pete van der Woude, editor extraordinaire, for working with me to strengthen my story.

To Natural History Unit Africa, and their associates Kira Ivanoff and Dale Hancock from the South African filmmaker Triosphere (who both used a still camera on occasion), for making available some of their photographs of me and the elephants, including the ones on the cover of this book. And to journalist Mark Stratton for allowing me access to some of his photographs too.

To the birds, bushbuck and vervet monkeys and their babies that kept me company as I wrote. And to the late Andy Searle, whose memory inspires me to keep at it.

JACANA

Other Jacana Media titles

The Elephants and I
Sharon Pincott

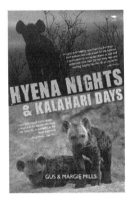

Hyena Nights &
Kalahari Days
Gus and Margie Mills

Insider's Guide
*Top wildlife photography
spots in South Africa*
Shem Compion

A Delight of Owls
African owls observed
Peter Steyn